Getting Along

Awareness activities that teach responsibility, self-respect, and respect for others

Anne W. Millyard and Rick Wilks

Fearon Teacher Aids
Simon & Schuster
Supplementary Education Group

We acknowledge with thanks the support of the Samuel
and Saidye Bronfman Family Foundation in the production of
this book.

Cover Design: Susan True

ISBN-0-8224-3377-X
Library of Congress Catalog Card Number: 80-65478
Printed in the United States of America.
1.9 8

Contents

Introduction

Getting Along addresses itself to all persons working with groups of children, be they in schools, public libraries, playgrounds, drop-in centers, youth organizations, in inner-city neighborhoods or small rural communities. Our particular concern is with groups containing kids* of differing social, economic, religious or cultural backgrounds. But whatever the group, all those working with kids have a common responsibility —to help young people cope with the business of developing a sense of self-in-the-world, a sense of growing up.

Children, by accepting themselves and their heritage, learn to respect their peers, to understand and tolerate differences and to appreciate and enjoy what they share: the experience of childhood (good and bad). We believe that with improved communication, social and racial tensions can be eased and a more harmonious climate created that will allow growth and the development of life skills. Children who are on the

---

*'Kids', we learned over the course of our work during the past four years, is the term most acceptable to children eleven and up. They would prefer not to be identified in any way other than as 'people', but barring that, 'kids' will do. As this book deals with 'children' and 'kids', both terms are used, each where it was deemed to be appropriate.

defensive, who are unsure of themselves and the roles they must play, will likely be passive. They will accept values that are inappropriate for their lives and not be able to take responsibility for shaping their futures. On the other hand, those who have built confidence and a sense of self-worth are better equipped to use their voice, to stand up for their rights and have some impact on their society. Children need to receive our confident message that they will grow up to be responsible adults who cope well, live with self-respect and contribute to their society.

In compiling the material for this book we have kept in mind the varying needs of children. While our main concern lies in the areas of cross-cultural communication and multi-culturalism, we have included activities that address themselves to the varied social and personal issues confronting children in general. Thus we have included a wide range of activities. There are settings for roleplaying, for those who express themselves by acting out; and discussions and writing activities for the more verbally inclined. Some ideas have been used successfully with groups of 8-year-olds and the more complex strategies with up to 15-year-olds. Most groups will be able to involve themselves with many of our suggestions on a level appropriate to their development.

We are conscious that this book is only a beginning; far from having all the answers, we are still seeking out the questions that have to be asked. We encourage you to adapt these strategies to the needs of your groups, and to use them as a basis for further invention.

Anne W. Millyard and Rick Wilks

1

Promoting Positive Interactions

Successful interaction in a group means, to us, that individuals are both giving and receiving. In the usual group, though, a few kids are so bent on expressing themselves that they cut everyone else out, and even interrupt each other. Others, with low self-esteem, never speak and have no expectation that they will be able to contribute. (Some hold back because they speak with a dialect or accent that has been ridiculed.)

In our work with kids, we establish order in discussions, so that good listening can take place. We also get all the kids to express themselves, since we know that always being cut out of participation creates anger and frustration, which in turn keeps a child from concentrating on what is being done or taught in the group.

THE CONCH OR SHELL TECHNIQUE

This technique was first developed by Dr. Rachel Pinney to facilitate communication between adversaries. We have adapted the method to suit our work with children's groups.

We all sit in a circle, either down on the floor or around a table, so that people face one another, no more than twelve at a time. The adult takes the role of coordinator rather than 'teacher' for these sessions. All present take equal responsibility for the teaching-and-learning experience. All are expected to contribute and usually do, no matter what the behavior normally may be.

A small object—a seashell, glass paperweight or anything delicate and pleasant to hold—is placed in the center of the circle. We suggest you pick your object carefully. Pencils may be pitched across the room. If you choose a delicate thing there is an implied responsibility to protect it. Speakers understand and usually respond well.

Anyone who wishes to make a contribution to the discussion must wait his or her turn to hold the shell, even if the person pauses to think or hesitates. No one grabs the shell from the person holding it, or reaches for it before it is again placed in the center. The coordinator also waits until the shell is sitting in the center to pick it up and speak, ideally when no one is waiting to take it. If things seems bogged down, the coordinator may suggest a 'round', where the shell is passed from hand to hand going around the circle. Kids may either pass it on without speaking or may take a turn. The shy and quiet-voiced kids thus receive and welcome the chance to be heard.

TEACH ME SOMETHING

This exercise is particularly suited to the kid with lower academic skills, the one who often feels excluded from successful participation in group activities.

If you ask your group to 'teach me something' you must be well organized about it. The situation to be avoided is: Adult says, "Teach me something," and the three or four most confident kids immediately rise to the challenge, showing you nifty tricks you have always wanted to know, while the rest of them are reinforced in their poor opinion of themselves, convinced that they can do none of these attractive things and never will. This would lead to a session of tall-tales telling, including, "You know what my uncle does?"

If you start this you must be prepared to continue it (part-time) for a period of several days to give *all* kids a chance to come up with something to teach you and feel good about themselves. Some of the most interesting skills we have we do not remember every day at the drop of a hat.

TAPE RECORDER INTERVIEWS

As we all know, children gladly tackle a difficult task as long as it looks like a game. A discussion will be rejected by some with the words, "Oh, I can't do that thinking stuff. That's boring." It turns out that Charlie can do that thinking stuff exceptionally well as you approach him (and the others) with a live tape recorder. Sample: "We are talking to Mr. Charles here on Front Street. Sir, I wonder if you would mind answering a few questions for a survey this station is conducting." Charles grabs the microphone and intones, "Certainly, as long as it doesn't take too long! I'm a busy man." "Thank you very much. We wondered how you feel about marriage. Should everybody be married?" While Charlie tells his peers that he has been married four times and has nineteen grandchildren, the others in the group look forward to their turn to be interviewed.

Have a list of questions ready that interest children, increasing in difficulty. If the group has decided that it is wrong to lie, ask 'Elvis Presley' or 'Helen Reddy' or Mary H., a police officer, if there might be a time when lying would be okay to help a friend or family member.

Other questions:
What age would you like to be?

What was it like when you were little?
What will you be like when you grow old?

('Old', you may discover, is 28 or 34, anything beyond that being apparently out of reach of the imagination for the young child.) We have discovered that children do not like to be asked what they expect to do or be when they grow up. Most have no idea and feel guilty about this.

TAPE RECORDER DRAMATIZATIONS

When school seems particularly difficult to cope with, children take comfort in remembering that the 'real world' (and thus, *most* of life) is tolerable and even fun. It is usually hard to get that real world into the classroom, in a way that makes it both a base for learning and keeps some of its enjoyable aspects available.

This is where we have had some success with tape recordings, acting out situations, choosing adult roles from a list you have prepared. (The kids may be too troubled to play themselves. Adults are a safe target here). Make sure you have a good variety of characters, commonly expected to cope well in difficult cir-cumstances. You will come up with a mountain of stereotypes — it does not matter. Have, for example, a plainclothes police officer, an ambulance attendant, a famous athlete, a taxi driver, a tourist (having been robbed), a witness to the calamity, a photographer and a reporter, any of these female as needed. Ask the kids to suggest others.

Ask for volunteers for just three roles. Give them the barest of plots to start with and let them go at it from there. They may be microphone-shy at first. Clowning with it helps to warm them up. Removing the tape may help too. Suddenly, it will work. There will be sub-plots and non sequiturs. Logic is not a requirement here, so at the height of confusion hand out all of the other roles at once. The non-talkers may be so taken in with the melee that most will participate one way or another, some as relaxed spectators. TV plot fantasies are released and shared in happy interaction.

At the end summarize, stressing the good things you saw as a spectator, making sure you give each kid credit for *something*.

Another time they may take turns with the microphone and

a. improvise (spoof) commercials,
b. do interviews,
c. make up a telephone conversation between two people

who have a wrong number,
who are not listening to each other,
who think they are talking to someone else.

It feels good occasionally to be allowed to exploit adult foibles, to make fun of self-important authority figures.

QUESTIONS FOR A TAPE RECORDER INTERVIEW

The following have worked well with groups eight years and up, in this case the interviewer being an older youth or adult. A similar series can be easily devised for other topics.

What is the difference between adults and children?
What are adults like?
Are adults perfect?
Do they know most of the answers?
Are they allowed to do what they want?
If not, why not?
*Do they have **more** or **less** freedom than children have?*
Who works at your house? Who else? Who else?

What do they do at work?

Does work have anything to do with money?

If so, in what way?

Is work for which people do not get paid, unnecessary work?

Is it unimportant work?

Is it more important work than the kind people get paid for?

Neither?

Do people with the highest pay for their work have the most important work to do? What kinds of work pay a lot of money?

Does this seem fair to you in all cases?

Think of a very important job in your community, one that seems really important to **you.** *Do you think the person who does this job earns a lot of money?*

Can you think of a person who does not earn much money but who has a very responsible job to do in your community?

2

Discussions
for Awareness

Good discussions usually result when kids introduce topics or controversial issues themselves. The involvement is intense and there is fun and excitement in exchanging opinions and developing critical thinking. This chapter introduces issues kids are bound to encounter. The setting is one in which they are able to discuss their feelings, anxieties or frustrations as well as joys with their friends or those directly involved in a shared activity. The exercises are designed to raise awareness as well as improve communication skills.

In many cases we only had to introduce the subject and heated debate resulted. However, in others kids were reluctant to begin or were influenced by one or several members of the group who presented a strong case for their point of view. In instances such as these we would enter the group, state that what we were about to say was an opposing argument to what was being presented in the group (it should be pointed out whether or not this is a personal point of view), and ask the group to consider these arguments.

If you are taking part in the discussion, make sure that the kids' arguments are directed at all members of the group and not just yourself. When discussion has resumed you may once again withdraw.

Discussions frequently result in creative writing. Kids are inspired to put their thoughts down in writing, after getting involved in a discussion and forming or altering solidifying opinions.

A TOPIC FOR STARTERS

We have found kids from age ten up always willing to trade views on the value of school, and its relationship to their goals and to the world of work. The following questions will usually serve to start a good active group exchange.

Suggestions:

If going to school were optional, would you go? Why or why not?

If yes, for how long, and what do you feel the school should do for you and you for it?

Are these things happening?

What would you do if you didn't come to school?

Should kids under sixteen be allowed to work instead of going to school?

What sort of work should kids be paid for?

Are there any subjects that you feel should be taught at school that are not on the curriculum? Are there any you are now taking that should not be included?

WHERE DO YOU STAND?

Ask your group of kids to stand in a line. Explain that each end of the line represents an extreme position, one end representing a strong 'yes' and the other a 'no'.

Select an issue about which the group feels strongly and ask them to find their place on the line. To determine their exact position they must negotiate with their peers. So, by discussing their own feelings on an issue in relation to those of their friends, kids will arrive at their appropriate place on the line.

After this has been done, divide everyone into two groups. To do this, match individuals with their counterparts until everyone has a partner.

For example,

1 2 3 4 5 6 7 8 9 10 11 12 13 14

Kids would be grouped as follows: 1 & 14, 2 & 13, 3 & 12, etc.

Now that you have set up pairs of people for discussion, you may proceed with a one-to-one discussion or form two groups and have a debate.

INSTALL A MIRROR

If you are indoors with your activities, whatever they may be, bring in a mirror. Make sure it is not the spy-in-the-drug-store variety. A good size, full length one is best. Next, encourage people, all ages, to stop and look at themselves every day. Look with them, convey what a pleasure it is, using a minimum of words. Support those in particular who quickly hurry past without looking at themselves.

On a particular occasion, get all the children together and discuss 'looking at oneself in the mirror'.

> *What do you see when you look into the mirror?*
> *Do you like looking into the mirror?*
> *Do you only do it when you are alone?*
> *Do you make faces at yourself in the mirror?*
> *Do you think other people look at themselves?*
> *Have you noticed that some people quickly look away when they suddenly see themselves in a mirror in public?*
> *Why do you think they do this?*

PEOPLE WHO ARE OLD

Many of the world's richer countries, including ours, have a large number of old-age homes, and large numbers of old people living in them. Is this something we should be proud of, or is it a problem? We have found many groups of kids ready to discuss this kind of issue, both because they feel it is important, and because it focuses on a somewhat remote part of society and the discussion is a little safer. Questions like the following are useful.

> *What does it feel like to be old?*
> *Do you know someone who is old?*
> *Have they changed over the years?*
> *How?*
> *Do you know much about their past lives?*
> *What were they doing when they were your age?*
> *Where did they live? What were their lives like?*
> *How do they feel about today's world?*
> *How would you like to spend your old age?*
> *Should people move in with their families?*
> *How do various cultures treat their old people?*
> *Do old people feel they are making a contribution to our society?*
> *What do you feel they may have to contribute?*

ROOTS: EXPLORING OLD WORLD VALUES

Before beginning this exercise you need to decide if it is appropriate for your community. We have found that there are people who do not wish their kids to participate in discussions on this topic, and who do not wish to delve into past experiences or disclose this kind of information to their children. Their feelings must be respected.

Have kids do some research into their family backgrounds, and then share information in discussion groups. Some items that can be explored are as follows.

> *What country did their family come from?*
>
> *What was it like there?*
>
> *What did their family do for a living, for entertainment?*
>
> *What were the problems and issues they faced? What choices were available to them to try to solve these things?*
>
> *What were they hoping for when they left their old country?*
>
> *Did they ever realize these things?*
>
> *How is their new country similar or different from the way they imagined it?*
>
> *Are the kids glad they decided to leave? Do the kids wish to stay put, or does the idea of living in another country appeal to them?*
>
> *If they were to leave, what country would they emigrate to? Why?*

MORE TOPICS FOR GROUP DISCUSSION

A series of three or more questions which builds in complexity seems to guide discussion in groups well. Those below are a few of the ones with which we've had success.

Hurts and Apologies

> *If someone does or says something that makes you feel really hurt, then later apologizes, can you forgive?*
>
> *Suppose **you** do something that hurts someone else, later you are sorry and apologize. Is it easy for you? Is it important enough for you to make yourself apologize?*
>
> *How do you act when someone else suggests you should apologize?*

National Diversity

> *Is there equality among all or most people living in the U.S.?*

Are all people equally accepted as Americans? If not, what people are fully accepted? What people not well accepted?

Should immigrants be encouraged to retain and continue to practice their life styles and customs?

Do you ever judge people by the way they speak? Do others?

The Future

What will be the world's/the U.S.A.'s/your community's/greatest problem when you are an adult?

Is there anything you can do about it?

Who else seems to understand that this thing is or is not going to be a problem?

Who can do something about it? What could they do?

You vs. Your Parents

What are some of the things your parents may have valued in their youth? What are some of the things they currently value? What are the reasons for the changes, if any? How does this compare with your list of values? How much do your parents' values influence yours?

How will your feelings be different (or similar) when you are old?

Will you be a different adult from those you now see? How?

Choices

If you had the opportunity to get people to read one book or see one television program, what would it be and why?

If there were reincarnation, as what would you come back? Why?

3

Examining Meanings

Kids' discussions become far more searching and interesting to them (as well as to teachers and others), when those involved are sensitive to the idea that language is not simple and precise. One person may attach a particular cluster of meanings and feelings to a term or statement, while the listener experiences quite a different cluster. Facts sometimes sound like opinions, opinions like facts. A speaker may be saying one thing and implying others. Awareness of these realities makes kids more careful listeners and questioners, as well as more sensitive observers of the speaker behind the words.

In this section we suggest a few approaches to examining implied stereotypes, discerning more general meanings amongst facts, and identifying hidden assumptions. The reader can go much further, and we encourage him or her to do so in this important area of learning.

DEFINING TERMS

An experience in values clarification may also begin with a discussion where the group defines words.

What is the 'judicial system'? Is it the same as 'justice'?
What is 'integrity'?
What is 'prejudice'?
What is 'obscene'? Who decides what is obscene?
What is 'bad taste'?

What is 'crazy'?

*What other words come to mind for any of the above? Do
you use these words? What words would you use
to express an opinion on an issue where any of these
would be a factor?*

We suggest that the coordinator stay on the sidelines
during this kind of discussion and let the group handle
it, using the creative listening method.

SUBTLE PEOPLE PUT-DOWNS

Following are several statements which contain subtle
implications about groups of people. Ask kids simply
whether there is anything the matter with each of
them. Then after some discussion, they may want to
find or create other such sentences. Trying to reword
or restructure the sentences is also instructive.

   a. My wife's grandmother and the other girls in
      her bridge club are coming over for lunch.

   b. That boy drove a cab while working on his
      college degree and then went right back to
      driving a cab.

   c. I think kids are cute. They say the funniest
      things.

If they like, kids can experiment with reading such
sentences in varying tones of voice and changing word
emphasis, to either make the implication very obvious
or to try and subdue it.

TRUE OR FALSE?

Challenge kids to tell which of the twelve sentences
below are 'true' and which are just opinion.

   a. Women are better able to look after children
      than men.

b. Violence on TV has no effect on the general population.

c. People from all countries are welcome in the U.S.A.

d. North Americans eat the healthiest diet in the world.

e. Joe Namath was the finest quarterback in football.

f. Geographically speaking, Canada is the second largest country in the world.

g. The Germans make better cars than the Japanese.

h. Clubbing seals over the head is a brutal way of killing them.

j. Driving a truck is a man's job.

k. Money is all one needs for happiness.

l. Money is the root of all evil.

How can we tell which is which?

What is the difference between 'fact' and 'opinion'?

Discuss fully.

IN THE NEWSPAPERS

As a group, select ten or twelve items of advertising from newspapers or magazines, then decide which ones are based on fact and which are rooted in unsupportable claims.

If fact, what is their source?

If opinion, whose is it? The advertiser's? That of a well-known personality appearing in the ad?

Look at the advertisements more closely. What small facts (the price of an item, for instance) can you find in several? What unstated ideas are carried by the drawing or pictures in the ad? What aspects are large or given strong treatment? What aspects are minimized?

Finally, look at a few news items, and decide how confident you are of the truth of various aspects reported.

GETTING MORE THAN THE FACTS

There are several levels on which one may perceive and analyze an issue or event. There is the 'facts level,' the 'concepts level' and the 'values level.' Focusing kids' attention on these levels separately will help them see the different kinds of meaning in material they may hear or read, and will help them listen more astutely in discussions.

To make the differences clear to a kids' group, it is helpful to go through one example, which at least some members of the group have shared with you or can share. This might be a discussion, a program on TV, an article in the newspaper. To illustrate the progression, we will relate at this time a discussion we saw on TV concerning the government's role in providing housing. The same kind of approach may be taken in the example you choose to discuss with the group.

On the facts level the following questions arose:

a. *How many people would like to make use of government subsidized housing?*

b. *Where is the housing being built?*

c. *How much will it cost to purchase these homes? To build them?*

d. *Who will maintain them?*

These are the sort of factual questions that are important in developing a basic understanding of an issue. While this level enables one to collect some necessary information, to achieve a real understanding of what is at stake we must delve somewhat more deeply into the matter. At this point we may consider the issue or event from the concepts level. For example:

a. *Why do some people feel it is necessary to have subsidized housing?*

     b. What are the main positive and negative social effects of this sort of housing?

     c. If we do not build subsidized housing, what are the consequences likely to be?

     d. How has this form of housing worked when tried in other areas?

When examining a subject from the conceptual level one looks at the causes and effects, the general principles involved and the relationship between the issues and other current issues as they affect society.

There is still one further perspective, this one being perhaps the most critical in forming a sense of what an issue is all about. On this level, the values level, one must become personally involved, take a stand, and relate the issues at stake to one's personal life. To return to the example:

     a. If you were to live in subsidized housing, how would you feel about it? If you do live in such housing, how do you like it?

     b. If you do not live in subsidized housing, have you ever visited someone who does live there? What impressed you about it? What did not?

     c. How would your life be different, if at all, should you move?

     d. Have you ever done anything to make your views on this subject known? What things might you do? Are there people already doing these things?

     e. If you were a resident making proposals for change what would some of your suggestions be?

When approaching an issue or event on the values level, it is almost necessary to personalize the questions to be considered. Only this step makes a person feel comfortable (or uncomfortable) with the realities being discussed, and only the realization of this comfort or discomfort leads to a true clarification of values for that person.

We suggest that this three-level approach is a sound one for considering and working out one's position on both personal and societal issues. This approach may also be used to examine history, newspapers, speeches and, to some extent, other people's actions.

ARE YOU CONVINCED?

Meaning is intentionally manipulated by those who set out to persuade us to their position, and kids cannot be expected to be careful listeners if they are not helped to be aware of some of the common techniques making up what can be called 'the art of persuasion.' The following speech, made by a ninth-grade student running for the office of Student Council President, contains many of these techniques. It can first be read to the group, discussed in general, and then discussed in terms of each of the persuasive techniques identified with capital letters. If desired, the speech can be duplicated and handed out after the kids listen to it the first time. Duplication makes it easier to analyze the specific techniques, which, in a speech like this, are successful partly because they are experienced so quickly. The listener is hard put to say what is 'fishy' about a particular technique before he or she must deal with the next.

Fitzgerald's speech to the student body:

I would like to open by discussing a very serious problem. It seems that there has been a rash of complaints about clothing being stolen from the boys' gym. Well, I would like to report that I just saw Mr. Kinsinger outside the office wearing a pair of very tight-fitting pants. You may draw your own conclusions. (A)

With the exception of these activities which are not part of the gym program, this school has a good record in the community. I want to keep it that way by representing you. If I become president, your ideas can be brought to me and will be put directly before the council. From whom could you get better representation without running yourself?

While it's true our school has a good record, I believe we can make it better. By joining together we can speak out against things we disagree with, no matter who's involved. Most of you whom I've talked to agree. Shouldn't you? (B)

I do not have all the answers, I'm not one of the top students in this school. My marks are not even the best. But is that what you want, a top student who will tell you what to do? I understand what's going on. I know the issues and your problems, I've been through many of them myself. This has given me a very intimate and thorough understanding of the issues at stake in this campaign. (C)

I think I've known most of you for at least three years. We've been through exams, Monday morning classes, showers after gym and Mr. Kanuski's math classes. These are things I wish I could change, but I don't think they would ever let me. (D)

So I will present my views on some of the issues. Let me begin by saying that many of my opponent's suggestions are ridiculous. (E) Take for example the cafeteria. Yeech! Please take the cafeteria. Anyone who has been to a half-decent restaurant knows where the caf food stands on a scale of one to ten. Something can be done about it. We could have better service, good food and the cafeteria could be a nice place to visit. I know people who don't enjoy lunch because of the current state of affairs there. Something can be done, but I must have your support. (F)

When I'm elected there will be further changes in the school. Some of my well-meaning but misinformed opponents have promised items such as a new juke-box for the caf. We all know this would be impossible, it would cost more money than we have. But, although it is totally unfeasible to purchase a new juke-box, I may be able to swing a deal on a good second-hand one. (G)

I don't think the issues have to be explained to you people. It's your school, you understand how it works (or doesn't), and you know what will make it a better place. I believe I speak for most of you when I say that one thing you would like to see is a better dance program. (H) My opponent has promised weekly dances. I expect these will be boring, poorly planned affairs. (J) I suggest bi-weekly dances with better quality groups or disc-jockeys. Each dance would cost more money, but by having fewer we could raise the quality of each one. A friend of mine who works at Radio Station KTIM has told me that he thinks this is an excellent idea and that he would be pleased to help us out whenever he's able to. (K)

There is another issue that I believe demands serious attention. It's that of the school budget. I'm sure that all of you know that you each contribute $1.50 to the student council. This sum, in addition to the amount contributed by the Board of Education, means that the council has $2,300 to spend each year. In the past what have you received for this money, your money? A year book, a few dances, and one or two clubs. I believe this money can be better spent, $2,300 is a great deal. Is it working for you? (L)

I think the future of this school promises to be a very exciting one. An improved cafeteria, more school dances, the juke-box; this will be a place students will be proud to attend, where people feel involved, and where they have a say. If we all co-operate there are many ideas we can implement. I want you to decide your own future. (M)

I know I have the support of most of you. I appreciate all the people who have approached me over the past few weeks to offer their help. Remember, if you support me wear the red and white buttons. There are more of us every day. (N)

I'm sure that there are many things you want that I haven't mentioned in this speech. If you come and talk to me I will have support in student council and can push your ideas through for you. (O)

Remember:

Go with a winner!
Go with experience!
Go with Fitzgerald! (P)

Fitzgerald did win the election. In a school of 1500 people he won by a margin of 46 votes.

Before you begin discussing the speech in detail, ask the kids if they were impressed by it overall. Also ask for general comments. The following questions will get the discussion started.

Did this person inspire confidence?

Was he credible (believable)?

Do you think Fitzgerald would make a good representative?

An honest representative?

Now help the kids examine the speech, referring to the sections indicated by the capital letters. Our comments on what Fitzgerald was doing follow:

(A) Using humor in a speech is a way of ensuring the audience is paying attention, even if it is only to wait for the next joke. People who tell funny jokes are well-liked, it is a way of winning friends. There is nothing wrong with this as long as the funny presentation does not cover up or make up for a lack of content in the speech. Have you ever laughed at a speaker and then wondered what it was all about when he or she finished? Do you think Mr. Kinsinger laughed at this joke?

(B) Here the candidate is trying to create an 'us' group. People like to feel part of the in-fashion crowd; there's comfort in numbers. People often use the rationale that if there is a large group that is in agreement, then their ideas can't be wrong. Certainly there is always the comfort of knowing that you will not be criticized by those around you. Furthermore, by creating the impression that there is a strong movement in a certain direction, the candidate is able to shake the confidence of anyone with opposing views, thereby causing them to re-examine their own beliefs.

(C) This may be termed the 'just plain folks' approach; it is one of the favorites in the art of persuasion. In this case the candidate attempts to convince his audience that he and his ideas are good because they are of 'the people', the regular folks, of which he is one. He tells people that he shares their experiences and feelings and therefore he understands their aspirations and problems.

Many elections turn into popularity contests, they may be a sign of who is better liked rather than who is the most qualified. The 'just plain folks' technique may be a ploy to win such a contest.

(D) There is a little of (B) and (C) in this paragraph, but also note the antagonism that is set up. 'Good guy' and 'bad guy' groups are created. In this 'us' and 'them' group structure the problems at stake are blamed on the 'thems'.

(E) This is a case of 'name-calling'. The candidate is attempting to give his opponent's ideas a bad label with the hope that this will cause us to reject or condemn the suggestions. Does he explain why he uses this label?

(F) He has cited the problem and no doubt all are in agreement that things in the caf are pretty deplorable, however, he never tells us exactly what he will do about it. By identifying the problem he has won our support, but to keep it he should have to solve the issue.

(G) In this case, even though he appears to have a solution for the juke-box question, he is still on shaky ground. By not citing concrete facts and figures we do not know how expensive the new juke-box would be, how much less his second-hand one will cost and where he is going to swing this deal. People must be held accountable for their claims. If they don't substantiate them, it may be that they are unable to.

(H) The candidate feels that it pays to compliment his audience, it makes them feel intelligent and perceptive.

It also shows that they are on the same wave length. Is he right?

(J) Is this another example of 'name-calling'?

(K) The testimonial. In this case the candidate is using someone who is respected to back his platform. Do you think this is an effective technique? Where else is it frequently used?

(L) He is leading the audience to inevitable conclusions by asking questions that have obvious answers. By doing this the listeners may believe that they have reached their own conclusions when in fact they have been led right to them. Figures or statistics are often used to strengthen a case.

(M) By painting a picture of a rosy future the candidate is inviting people to vote for him so that this desirable vision will become a reality.

(N) This is the 'bandwagon' technique. He is saying that everyone — at least all of 'us' — is doing it; he hopes that the listeners will feel that they too should follow the crowd and 'jump on the bandwagon'. This is somewhat like (B) in that the candidate is trying to foster a desire for membership in an 'us' group.

(O) One of the oldest techniques in the world; the unfounded or blind promise. The 'tell me what you want and I'll do it for you' promise ignores most of the realities of any political system by assuming that the elected official is all-powerful.

(P) The slogan. The candidate attempts to create a positive image that will stay in people's minds, especially when they go to vote.

This candidate made use of only some of the common techniques of persuasion, and of course speeches are only one form in which these techniques may appear. All of us have some contact with the art of persuasion each day of our lives, either as a recipient, or as users, as we try to make a point to someone else. If kids are prepared to spot these techniques as they arise, they will not be nearly as vulnerable. Their defenses may be even higher if you remind them that when people employ the art of persuasion they are almost always wanting to sell something; it may be a philosophy, a bar of soap, or themselves. This desire will be foremost in their minds, meaning that the truth is subordinated to effectiveness.

ASSUMPTIONS BASED ON LOOKS

Another potential distorter of meaning is the assumptions that we make about people, based on only first impressions, and often on looks. Those assumptions may then color our later understandings of what these people say, or do. You can help kids become more sensitive to this problem by finding four photographs of individuals you know but that they do not. Ask the group to rate each person on the following characteristics. The ratings may be written down:

How likely that this person would be your friend.

Things you think you'd like about them.

Things you think you'd dislike about them.

Then, give the group each person's name, and a brief description of each. You might tell about the person's educational experiences, work, family roles, and the like. Ask kids to rate the people again, using the same questions. Discuss how the people's names and interests may have influenced the later judgments. Finally, discuss questions like these:

How are facial, and other visible characteristics including skin color, apt to affect your opinion of someone?

If someone were to see just your picture, what would he or she say about you?

4

Values
Challenges

Many of the topics treated in this book are good for
helping kids clarify their values about a wide range of
aspects of their lives and their world. The strategies
recommended in this chapter are those most readily
usable as models. That is, their form can be used for
helping groups approach a variety of subjects. They
are alike in that they ask participants to make at least
a hypothetical commitment to a value or a priority. This
ensures that the ideas worked with are not just intel-
lectually understood, but are incorporated into kids'
feelings and perceptions, at least at some level.

WHAT WOULD YOU DO DISCUSSIONS

In 'what would you do' discussions it is important to
convey the message that there is no one proper answer.
The question ideally invites kids to examine all the
options. Also, it is important to mention to them that
one really never knows what exactly one would do at a
given moment under certain circumstances; the question should read: "What would you hope to do?" or
"What do you think you might do?"

In the following examples the burden of responsibility in 'getting involved' varies greatly. It is left up to you
to decide which examples are suitable for the group you
work with.

a. You are walking into a subway station or department store with a friend. You are on your way to an important event. You are a little late. As you go down the escalator you notice a young woman carrying a small baby on her arm coming up the opposite escalator. She is crying, sobbing loudly in fact.

How does this make you feel?

Why do you think she might be breaking down?

Is it best to leave her alone or to offer her help or sympathy? If so, how?

b. For the second time in two years a person in your neighborhood has, either deliberately or carelessly, caused unnecessary suffering to a wild animal. The animal got away, still in pain.

Do you get involved? If so, how? Do you tell the person? Do you discuss it with your parents? If they feel that your action in the matter would have a bad effect on your neighborhood relationships, would you change your mind?

c. Walking at a shopping plaza with a member of your family you see an old lady coming toward you with her dress all crumpled up in front and her underwear showing. She is not aware of it.

Is it anyone's responsibility to tell her?

Should she be left to discover it herself?

Which would embarrass her the least?

d. You are waiting in a long line-up of kids at a fair or movie theatre. The line is moving slowly. A big man comes up and shoves his son into the line in front of you. Everybody sees it. The boy is uncomfortable.

What are your choices?

What would be the easiest thing to do?

What do you think you would do?

e. Imagine you are waiting somewhere and you see a younger or smaller child treated unfairly in public. In a store, for instance, the child may be ignored or pushed out of a line-up.
   Do you feel the urge to help out in some way?
   Do you get involved? If so, how?

PROBLEM-IDENTIFICATION CHALLENGES

Often the complexity of real situations makes the various value-stakes involved very hard to figure out, and practice at this task in discussion is something that most kids need. The following story can be read as a true personal experience, or another one, similar in complexity, can be made up.

The other day I was riding the bus at a quarter to nine in the morning on my way to work. At each stop groups of kids boarded the bus on their way to school, and it was soon extremely crowded. People were jammed in doorways and could not step up past the driver, let alone back into the bus. Tickets and tokens were handed along and dropped into the box by passengers next to it.

At one stop several people left the bus, so that those who boarded last could move on in. Several boys in their teens walked to the center of the bus which was still very crowded.

At a stop street the driver brought the bus to a halt and said to one of the boys, "Are you going to put your ticket into the box?" "I paid," said the boy. "You didn't pay. You were back there at the door, and you didn't get near that box," said the driver. "I passed my ticket to my friends here and they put it in for me," protested the boy. "They put in their own ticket, nothing for you," said the driver. The two boys with the accused spoke up. "He paid. I'm telling you," one of them said in a loud voice. "I'm not moving this bus till you pay your fare or you get off," said the driver sternly. The boy just stood there and his friends started to snicker.

No one made a move. All the passengers kept quiet. I sat in my seat wondering who was right. Was this boy in the habit of playing little games with bus drivers on his way to school? He seemed sincere enough to me. Were kids in the school up the street taking advantage of the crowd and the confusion in the mornings to get free rides? Could the driver really tell from where he sat whose tickets had been passed along?

The bus was still not moving. All the kids would be late for school and the adults late for work. Tension was building.

"I don't even have any money on me," mumbled the boy to his friends. "My mother is going to take me to the dentist at noon. She's picking me up . . . " The driver began talking at the same time, starting the bus. He told the boy in the future he would be required to personally *show* him his ticket.

It was my first day on this job. I was very uncomfortable being late. All the kids left the bus together and had a short walk down a side street. It was nine o'clock.

> *What was the problem?*
> *Whose job was it to take responsibility here?*
> *Who had the power in this situation?*
> *Anyone else?*
> *Was this situation resolved fairly?*
> *Should I have taken an initiative?*
> *If so, what kind and how?*
> *Would this story be any different if the bus driver had
> suspected an **adult** had not paid?*
> *Was it more important that the adults be on time than
> the kids?*
> *Vice versa?*

What would you hope to have done?
Have you ever been in a situation like this?
   What happened?

SELF-DISCOVERY

Ask members of the group to arrange the following educational goals in order of priority to them:

   a. acquiring basic skills;
   b. gaining factual information;
   c. learning to get along with others;
   d. learning critical thinking;
   e. learning how to learn;
   f. learning how to compete;

Then ask them to name five other items of importance to each of them individually, and arrange those in order of priority. Each person should look at both of the lists, and ask "What have I discovered about myself?"

THE VALUES AUCTION

The object of the values auction is to provide an accepting environment that encourages kids to sort out their own values, gain insights into the reasons why others may differ and re-examine their own opinions. No matter what the intellectual response to the auction is, this is an exercise kids always enjoy and frequently request to do again. For the auction we prefer to work with twelve to fifteen kids who are grouped in threes or fours. Each group is assigned a letter of the alphabet and awarded a total of 500 points for the bidding. In addition, each group has a pencil and one sheet of paper.

The kids are then asked to imagine themselves in a position of influence that would enable them to effect changes in their community or society. Invite them to think of things in their lives that trouble or anger them, then offer them the opportunity of changing those things. We never suggest an example. They should think of plausible alterations or alternatives; no one may change the sky to yellow because that would please them. Areas of change may involve their family, street, school, community or country.

Members of any of the groups should think of changes they would like to see and offer their idea to the coordinator. These suggestions are then written down by each group and the coordinator. You may wish to collect 10 to 12 items. We do not show approval or disapproval for any of the suggestions as we do not wish to influence the kids' opinions. Items should come from different people so that the list reflects as many interests as possible. You will find that suggestions cover a wide range of items such as 'Lower prices for chocolate bars', 'Down with women's lib', 'Lower taxes' or 'Bring back capital punishment'.

When the list is complete a pre-auction conference is held within each group to determine the collective stand on the issues. The kids are to discuss the items and decide which ones are priorities and which are not as important to them. They may decide that only one is of major concern or that seven of the items are of special importance. This is a very important part of the exercise, for it is in this stage that kids will have to explain, defend or convince others of their point of view. When each group has determined their priorities they are ready to begin the auction.

However, first explain that no group may bid more than their 500 points. They must allocate them according to how important they feel an item is. Of course, only the group that makes the highest bid surrenders the points. Emphasize that the objective is *not* to collect as many items as one can for the group, but rather to show support for their priorities. Bids rise by 10 points to avoid an extremely long auction. In addition, we stipulate that the group must be in agreement before a bid is offered. You should not auction the items in the order they have been written down; this will prevent participants from 'unloading' their points on the final item.

Each item is now auctioned off by the coordinator. When this has been completed read back to the groups the items that collected the highest bids. This will show them what their priorities are.

The final, and perhaps most important, part of the auction is the discussion that follows. This should take two courses: You may wish to discuss any controversies that arose. Using the creative listening technique allow the kids to air their views. Secondly, it is important to discuss what the groups can do now that they have identified their priorities. In what ways can they work to make their desired changes a reality? To whom can they speak? Would writing letters help? What can they do in their day-to-day lives? Where can they collect more information?

The auction may be repeated with a change in purpose. Instead of thinking of changes, you may ask them to focus on things they value, things they hope to preserve and keep. Or you may ask them to suggest things that they feel they are expected to like or respect, then compare this with the list of items they value.

You may find it of interest to repeat the auction some weeks or months later. Have the kids altered their view-points in any way? Have their priorities changed?

Discuss fully.

5

Settings for Roleplaying

When kids are encouraged to go beyond discussion of 'what would you do' or 'how would you behave' questions, and instead imagine situations and act their way into the feelings involved, you'll find that intense involvement is almost always the result. And there is value in living a situation, through roleplay, from a vantage point quite unlike the one a person usually maintains. In this section, a variety of approaches to roleplaying are provided, some quite open-ended and personal, others oriented to experiential understanding of a particular issue.

THE MOST IMPORTANT PERSON

Ask children to imagine they are talking to the most important person in their individual lives. What would be some of the thoughts on their minds?

It is interesting that many children have real trouble pin-pointing 'the most important person' in their lives. They suggest parents, sisters and brothers, God. Those who say, "I would be talking to myself!" are sometimes made to feel guilty for such self-centered ideas by the group and subsequently withdraw from their original choice, making strenuous efforts to be heard by the adult who introduced the discussion. The most important task for the adult is to keep the environment accepting, to remain non-judgmental, yet attentive.

ACTING OUT ROLES

Become one of the following:

a. an important person;
b. a reasonable person;
c. a jealous person;
d. a person feeling remorse;
e. a scared person.

Now put them all together in a scene as

a. people in a family;
b. a group of friends.

What happens? Play it out first, then write the story or scenario.

HELP WANTED

One person in the group becomes the owner of a small appliance store. Business has been brisk the past few months, so you are considering an expansion. However, this means hiring additional staff. It is a small store and you will be working closely with your new staff member. The following people have answered your newspaper advertisement:

a. A student who is a recent graduate from a community college. She has some sales experience, but not in the appliance field. She is anxious to work.

b. A middle-aged man from India who used to be a partner in a small electronics shop.

c. A woman who has just had a child and is anxious to have a job. She used to work as a psychologist but left to have her baby. Now she wants to find whatever sort of work she can.

d. An old friend hears that you have a position open. He has been out of work for a few months and would like to work with you. He has served a short time in prison where he learned how to fix light machinery.

Each member of the group plays one of the above roles. First they should develop a resumé and then apply for the job. The store owner shall arrange and conduct an interview with each person.

Upon completion of the interviews the shop owner should write a letter or have another meeting with each applicant to explain his decision.

Afterwards you may wish to discuss why certain approaches were more successful than others.

a. *Should the applicant's need for a job be a factor the employer should consider?*

b. *Do people from other countries stand less of a chance of finding work? If so, why?*

c. *How much does appearance matter when seeking work?*

US AND THEM

This exercise juxtaposes a person's self-perceptions (asked for first in the preparatory questions) to his or her perceptions of others, then provides for a roleplay if the kids seem to be considering "me" and "them" as very different, or in opposition.

Use these questions to start:

What makes you happy?
How do you feel right now?
What are you like?
What are other people like?

Are there people who are different from you? If so,
how are they different? Where do they live?

Sometimes surprising misconceptions about groups
and other nationalities emerge in such discussions.
When this happened, we invited the children holding
particularly negative views about 'them' to play out a
dialogue they made up themselves, between

    a. two of 'them',
    b. one of 'them' and one of 'us',
    c. two of 'us' and one of 'them',

then to switch roles. Make a point of asking them to
pretend they are adults in one session, then children in
another. The difference in dialogue and tone will be
dramatic. Also, the 'bad guys' will become increasingly
more 'like everybody else'. Discuss fully.

METAMORPHOSIS
(with apologies to Franz Kafka)

We introduce this exercise by telling children about
Franz Kafka, the Austrian novelist who died in 1924,
and his influence on modern literature. In THE TRIAL,
THE CASTLE and other novels, Kafka depicted human
beings as hunted and haunted by anonymous powers.
Not able to understand how these mysterious powers
control their lives, his characters only knew that these
forces were invisible and impersonal. They took the
shape of documents, machines and bureaucratic red
tape, all of which work to control people's actions.

His literary style was to present nightmarish events
in crisp and factual language, heightening the readers'
sense of suspense and bewilderment. His story
METAMORPHOSIS deals with a man who goes to bed
at night and wakes up to find that he has changed into a
man-sized cockroach.

We suggest to the children that we might all imagine

that upon waking up in the morning we find we have turned into another person.

It might be a good idea to tie this exercise into a study of other cultures. In a library program or camp this exercise could be preceded by reading Indian or Inuit legends to bring in information that is shared by all. This will enable the children to be more comfortable with the roleplaying situation.

Here are a member of possibilities to vary the exercise.

Imagine you wake up and have turned into

    a. a person of the other sex;
    b. a person you would like to be;
    c. a person who lives in another country or continent;
    d. a person you would be afraid to be;
    e. a person who does not understand you.

Sitting in a circle, we close our eyes for a few minutes to get completely involved with the role, then we talk about waking up as that other person. We then describe how we feel, how people react to us, how our lives are now different and what we must do to cope.

IMAGINE YOU ARE ON A BUS

Imagine you are on a bus with a lot of other people and the following happens:

One person insults and pushes another person around;

One person looks on in approval;

One person puts out his hands as if to interfere, then withdraws;

Two persons look horrified but do nothing;

Two persons pretend nothing is happening;

One person speaks to the person doing the pushing;

One person is being insulted and being pushed around.

If you were playing out the scene on the bus, which role would you have? (Let them act it out if they wish).

What would your feelings and thoughts be?

What would have to happen to make you take one of the other roles?

Are there any possible roles not described here?

What might they be and what would such people be doing?

Discuss fully. Avoid showing a negative reaction to the kid who says, "I was normal. I minded my own business." Ask the group in an even voice, "Why do normal people mind their own business?"

'PUTTING DOWN'

The group of children is divided into two groups; the Greens and the Blues. The Greens should have at least three-quarters of the children, that is, in a group of twenty, fifteen should be Greens. The remaining members of the group are Blues.

Instructions for Greens:

You are a strong majority of the population. You are a well-established group, you have been together for many years and have become close friends. You do almost all your day-to-day activities together. You like being a member of the Green group, you are surrounded by your friends and you are pleased that you are not a member of the Blues.

In fact, you do not get along with Blue group members. You sometimes talk about them with your friends, but you do not really know any of them. You only see them passing by, at which time you might say hello.

Instructions for Blues:

You are a much smaller group and because of this you must be nice to the Greens. You try to be friends, but never with great success. You do not get your way very often; things are done the way Greens want to.

Scenario:

Long ago the Greens started wearing paper arm bands of any color. They said this was because they thought they looked good, but in reality they wore them to show people they were not members of the Blues. All Greens should wear the paper arm band.

The coordinator sets a certain situation (one that the children are likely to have encountered), i.e. we suggest that you try a party or a game of catch. If you like the former idea, tell the children they are at a class party at someone's home which is being held to celebrate the end of the school year. Both groups have been invited and all the children will attend.

The coordinator sets a certain situation, one that the children are likely to have encountered. We suggest standing together talking and laughing. The Blue group is also together, but in a different part of the room.

The Green group are planning some activities to conduct at the party. So far they have only discussed their ideas among themselves, no invitation has been issued to the Blues.

Begin the party with the Green group planning out things to do. The Blues must decide how they will respond. The participants are then instructed to act out the scene keeping in mind their assigned attitudes.

The time limit is left up to the discretion of the coordinator, but remember that role-playing situations should last only long enough to make a point. If they are too long they become potentially destructive.

Follow-up discussion:

    a. Did the groups integrate? Why or why not?

    b. In what ways were the Blue group 'put down' by the Greens?

    c. How did the Blues respond?

d. Did this response have any effect on the Greens?

e. How did it feel to be 'put down'?

f. How did it feel to 'put down' someone else?

g. Have you ever felt the way people in the Green group said they felt? What about the people in the Blue group?

h. Do you think many people in our society feel 'put down'?

j. What can they do about it? What can **you** do about it?

THE ANNUAL INTERNATIONAL TRACK AND FIELD MEET

This game focuses on our response to cultural differences.

Divide the children into two equal groups, no more than fourteen participants altogether. Give the first group the welcoming committee's (hosts') scenario to read. Tell them you will return to answer their questions. Go to the second group (in another room or area) with the scenario for the visiting athletes. Instruct them together. It is a good idea to have them practice their roles for a moment after you answer their questions and while you return to the first group.

If you can have juice and cookies as props this does help children get involved in their roles. Some of them may have only a vague notion of what an 'official reception' might be like. When ready have the visiting athletes arrive. The party should not last longer than ten minutes.

End the party and start the follow-up discussion. First focus on the group of hosts and ask how they felt in their roles.

Was it easy?

Did the visitors respond readily to their efforts?

Were they fun to talk to?

What did they learn?
Then turn to the visitors:
Were they made to feel comfortable in this country?
Did they feel welcome?
Were there any difficulties?
Would they like to live here?
If not, why not?
Discuss fully.

The coordinator's responsibility is to let the children discover how newcomers may feel when coming here, and why. Some of the participants may recall how they or their families felt when they did arrive. Once, when we had an opportunity to video-tape the session, children were extremely surprised when confronted on the screen with their own non-verbal behavior.

Scenario: Welcoming Committee (Hosts)

You are a group of young athletes who have been chosen by your government to represent your country, and to welcome the visiting athletes from a number of foreign countries. The official reception, a party to greet the young guests, is held at the airport after their arrival.

You have been told to do your best to make the foreign athletes feel comfortable. They have never been to this country before but all speak English very well. Think of ways to make them feel welcome. Remember, they will judge this country by the way you behave.

Scenario: Visiting Athletes (to be sub-divided into four groups)

    a. You are (a) young sprinter(s) from TABOR, visiting this country for the first time. You have been told before leaving that your country would be judged abroad by the way you behave, so you have to be *very* polite at all times. In your country it is *not* polite to look directly at people when talking to them. During this party you look straight down on the floor when talking to your hosts.

b. You are (a) high jumper(s) from IBIDA, and you are coming here for the first time. You speak English very well. In IBIDA people are very friendly with each other. They stand *very close* to the person they are talking to. You are trying to be very friendly to make a good impression and remember to stand really close to the person you will be talking to at the forthcoming party.

c. You are on the relay team from MONTISI. You are very proud to have been chosen to run in this international event and you are anxious to be very polite. In MONTISI people touch each other a lot. They hold their partner's hand while talking to him or her, or touch each other on the shoulder or arm. You want your hosts to think well of you, so you touch them all the time.

d. You are (an) athlete(s) from SYLVANIA. In your country it is an old tradition to *never* interrupt people. This is to show that you are polite and listening to what is being said. You go so far in SYLVANIA as to wait for 15 seconds before answering another person's questions to show him or her that you are carefully considering it. So you try to be extra polite and count to 15 (by yourself) before speaking to your host.

6

Stories for Problem Solving

The story session is, of course, one of the oldest and most successful interactions between adult and child that produces good, warm feelings of love and attention, of community. It is an opportunity to exchange information and may generate relaxed conversation or heated debate. Stories create situations that children relate to. They use their own resources to solve the real-life conflicts presented in our open-ended stories.

On the following pages we supply a variety of true stories and a few that are realistic fiction (confirm those that are true), designed for different group needs. We wish to point out that there are no 'suitable boys' and girls' stories' here. If there are eight girls and three boys in a group we definitely use the Hockey Story, and if numbers are reversed, deliberately expose boys to a story with a typical dilemma facing girls individually or in groups. This helps sensitize them to the situation of the other sex.

We either read or tell the open-ended story as if we intended to present it all. The message is that yes, of course, there is an end to this story. Once you have covered all the information that introduces the characters and their conflict situation you can stop anywhere, or, as in the case of the Hockey Story, tell what happened in the end and ask them to think of a solution to the problem the group faced in the middle of the story in order to arrive at the happy ending.

While the purpose of much of our work is to reduce tensions among groups of children from different cultural backgrounds, *we avoid pinpointing* and thereby limiting a character in a story. We may be talking about a black child from Jamaica and what happens to him or her, but if we describe the child's *situation* and some of the *reactions* and *feelings* rather than physical features more of the others in the group will have an opportunity to identify with his or her problem. If the discussion of possible turns in the story and the isolation of the central problem are just not forthcoming at all while you sit back and listen (and you should be very relaxed about your expectations and make it clear that there is all the time in the world to work this out), then you may wish to suggest that *people play out the various roles* in the story. If there are only three roles and eleven children, tell them right away that you will do it three times, or invent extra children's roles to bring pressure on the sidelines. Do not introduce adult characters if the story does not contain any. It will be interesting to observe whether or not the children themselves simply bring in adult authority figures to quickly solve all the problems.

Do not let the children change the story base to escape from the conflict. Some groups are so uncomfortable with one another that they try to avoid the task by clowning or satirizing the situation to keep it safely 'out there', away from their own feelings. It may be a certain ostracized child in the circle whose presence embarrasses them. Role-playing helps in these cases. Amazingly, those who said the most harsh and punitive things about the 'bad guy' in the beginning often volunteer to play him or her, and find genuine human and revealing dialogue for this character. It is this process, observed by all the people in the group, that helps

children, little by little, get rid of the notion that there
are others who deserve our prejudice because of their
color, cultural background or innate evil nature. If two
boys out of three playing the 'bad kid' come in with
snarls, shifty behavior and artificial sounding dialogue (we do not interrupt this presentation), invariably the third one will reveal in his acting that a nine-
year old stealing a bike may be just anyone down the
street who probably acted on an impulse and cannot
handle the trouble he stumbled into.

It is important to leave time for a summing-up discussion at the end.

Did they like the people in the story?
*"What did you just learn from each other? I think I
learned . . ."*

In order to encourage kids' critical thinking, and
work towards sensitization to the other person's needs
and feelings it is most important to vary approaches.

Whether you work with kids in a school, public
library program, summer camp or neighborhood drop-
in center, we found it not advisable to follow one
strategy for too long just because it worked well the first
time. It would be a mistake, for example, to bring in a
succession of stories dealing with depressing disasters
to improve problem-solving skills. Many kids lead
painful private lives and they will quickly react with,
"Brother! Not another sob story!"

This is why we have included some sample stories
that have no immediate relation to kids' problems
today. You will find that kids are quite eager to involve
themselves with an ancient fable and the underdog in
it. They will be able to discuss willingly the plight of
adult poor, oppressed people, the many obstacles they
faced and other aspects — way back then. Encourage
them to think of ways in which people might stand up
for themselves, ways that work, ways that would bring
about improvement of a permanent nature. Stress your

belief that the individual and people working together can indeed have a strong and positive impact in society.

STEVE IS BUYING A MOTORCYCLE

Steve is sixteen. He has a decent job in a garage. He likes the people there and they respect him. He does a good job and is reliable.

Steve has just bought a second-hand motorcycle. It has been in an accident and needs repairs, but it is a Harley-Davidson and he could not have afforded it any other way. He is paying it off bit by bit. His mother co-signed the loan. He sends a check to the bank every month. He has to make his payments on time or they will take his Harley back. Steve always makes his payments and mails them at the post office.

One day he gets a call at the garage from a woman at the bank where he borrowed the money. She says they did not get his check and he has to pay up right away. He tells her that he mailed it the previous Friday, as always. She says she will check again but it did not get to her. Steve is pretty upset. He knows he made the payment and dropped it into the mail as usual. In the afternoon she calls again and says they did not get the check and that he must send the money right away.

In his lunch hour Steve goes over to the post office and asks what could have happened to his letter with the check. They are not very happy to see him. They are busy. Did he mail it registered? No? Is he sure he mailed it on that particular day? They say they will look into it, but he feels that they are trying to get rid of him. So he goes to his boss and tells him about the whole thing. The boss says he can go to the bank and stop payment on his first check. That costs money, at least $2.00. Then he has to make out another one, that costs money again and postage for mailing. He tells Steve to write to the post office to complain.

How would you handle this situation?

How do you find the person to write to and how do you write a complaint?

If it seems difficult and time-consuming would you perhaps decide not to do it and forget about it?

HOCKEY STORY

Steve Rodgers had been doing this for years, ever since he had started playing goal. He was the same age as the rest of the kids, 11, but a bit shorter.

They all played hockey every Saturday morning at 9:00 and they played all day long, in the middle of the street. They always played the same way. Steve was in goal and the two girls on the team played defence with him. The other three boys were taking shots on goal. There were not enough kids to have two teams.

This morning the puck (actually, it was an old tennis ball), rolled along the rough pavement and one of the offensive players delivered a beautiful wrist shot. It went high and in just under the crossbar. Before anyone could say anything, Steve batted it out of the net.

"What a save," he yelled.

"SAVE?!" screamed the boys. One of the girls turned and said, "I think it was in, Steve, really it was." Their goalie disagreed. He went into his usual demonstration of how he made the save. The boys yelled at him and waved their sticks around. The girls sat down on the curb to see if Steve would go home to his mother to complain again, or would calm down and they could go on.

Steve's face was red. He turned his back on them and leaned on the crossbar. The boys waited. Then they started pleading with him to go on playing. Gary raised his voice:

"Okay, guys. Let's say Steve made the save as he says." One of the girls nodded. The boys started to protest, then shrugged.

"Okay, same old story. Puck goes in, but we don't score . . . "

So they went on playing. Steve made some saves. When he made a really good one, the defence praised him. Suddenly, the ball just sort of slowly rolled into the corner of the net past Steve and stayed there. The boys looked at the girls. The girls looked at Steve. He batted it out angrily, picked up his net and started walking home.

Gary threw his stick way up in the air. He was really mad.

"Why do we have to put up with this cry-baby," he yelled.

"For one thing because nobody else wants to play goal," said the girls. "We do so," the boys insisted. "He won't let us use his net or pads."

Just then two of the kids from the south side of the school came over, carrying new sticks and a puck. They were a year older, but had not been playing much hockey until now. The kids could tell by watching them at recess.

"We had an idea," called Tony. "How would you guys like to get together next week for a game? We've got a net now and all, so-" "Hey, great," Gary said, but the girls hesitated. "Can we let you know at school Monday?" they asked. "Oh, okay," said Tony after a moment and then left. "What are we going to do about Steve?" "Yes, are we going to help him cheat or what?"

The kids did get together the following week. The game ended in a tie.

What did the kids do, in your opinion, to make things work out?

Is this strictly a hockey problem?

Does any one person have more of a difficulty than the others?

Should they ask an outside person to come and help?

If so, what kind of a person?

If there is no outside person, what should they do?

Does not-playing-any-more solve anything?

Can you think of another ending to the story?

One answer:

They found an impartial kid who acted as referee. Steve promised to accept his rulings and did. They all had fun.

THE BICYCLE STORY

Grant has moved to this city with his parents. He is about the same age as you kids. His family came from another country, but he speaks English quite well.

At first they lived in a small town and in his other school Grant did not have any friends. He had problems. In any case the kids were picking on him. He did some things there he wishes he had not done. Now his family is happier. This is a nice place. He likes his new neighborhood. His parents both like their jobs. His new school seems just fine. He has been there for a week now. So far he has not made any friends here either, but then he came in the middle of the school year, in April. Other kids had formed friendships already. There is one boy, Peter, who has been pretty nice to him, though. He talks to him at recess and seems friendlier than the others. Grant is hoping that they will be friends. He is looking forward to the weekend. Perhaps they will go to the park and throw the ball around or do something else together.

This is Friday and that day something happens that puts Grant in a difficult position. A bicycle is stolen from the school yard, Sam's brand-new bike. The principal announces it before most of the kids have left for lunch, and from the way the people in the halls are acting Grant has to come to the conclusion that they think he stole the bike. No one comes out and accuses him openly, so he cannot defend himself. But kids stop talking as he passes them and even the adults look funny as he comes along. Grant is very upset. The reason he is really upset is that he thinks he saw his new friend, Peter, bicycle away from the school yard at recess. Grant is pretty sure Peter told him earlier in the week that he does not have a bike.

On his way home for lunch Peter thinks about the problems he is facing.

Who has the most serious problem in the story?
What is it and what are some other problems?
Should Grant turn to anyone else for help?
If so, to whom? Why?
Pretend you are doing a play about this situation. Which one of the parts would you choose?
How about playing out the parts and looking for a good ending as you go along? Now switch parts.
Did this change the story?
Can you remember a similar experience of your own where a satisfactory/not so satisfactory solution was found?

In the real, true story Grant went to Peter and offered to help him return the bike to the school yard early Monday morning (after first finding out that Peter really did take the bike). They did return the bike together. Sam reported to the principal that he found it there in good condition. The principal asked Sam if he wanted her to find out who did it and punish this person. Sam thought about it for a moment and then he said no, he did not really need to know who did it, as the bike was back and in good shape. The principal told Sam it was fine with her and they left it that way and forgot about the whole thing. Grant and Peter became friends.

Kids always ask us about the ending in the *real* stories. They are very pleased when they hear that it is close to what they came up with on their own. Often they find superb and imaginative solutions themselves that enrich the story. Occasionally a kid will say, "If I were Peter and I had taken that bike, I would need to tell someone about it eventually. I would feel too bad about it." It is important to acknowledge kids' feelings in these stories.

RONNIE'S CHOICE

In order to show that he too has some smart new clothes, Kevin decides to steal a sweater just like the new one that Jarvis has received. He visits a large department store where he spots the one he wants. But the store is crowded and he is not sure that he can take it without being seen. So he leaves and enters a small store down the street where the manager is the only person present. Just as Kevin is depositing a sweater in a shopping bag, his friend Ronnie walks in and sees the theft.

Kevin makes his hasty exit as the manager turns around. She sees Kevin running out of the store and immediately becomes suspicious. It takes only seconds for her to notice that a sweater is missing. Several articles of clothing have been stolen over the past month and she is angry to see it happen again. Realizing that Kevin is well on his way she grabs Ronnie and tells him he will get into trouble unless he reveals his friend's name. Ronnie thinks over his choices.

   a. He should not tell. All stores expect to have some rip-offs. Kevin is a friend and telling would destroy the friendship, while not telling would probably ensure an even stronger relationship because Kevin would be grateful to him.

b. He ought to tell. He was not responsible, it was Kevin's business. He stole, he must take the risk of being caught. Why should he get into trouble for something he did not do? Besides, this is a small store that can't afford the loss, unlike the larger department stores.

c. He should not tell. The store owner has done nothing for him, there is no mention of a reward so it would not be right for him to help out by giving Kevin's name. He has done nothing and he does not wish to be involved, it can only bring him trouble.

d. He should tell for everyone's sake. Stealing is a crime, it is wrong. We all have to obey the laws or our society cannot continue to exist. Kevin has responsibilities as a citizen in this society. We cannot ignore the laws when it pleases us.

Discuss Ronnie's choices and advise him what to do by imagining you are one of the following people:

a. the manager of the store;
b. Kevin;
c. a policeman;
d. Ronnie;
e. Kevin's parents;

What is your own view?

THE VISIT

A friend of yours, Kim Kohl, has just returned from a visit to Taleah with her family. She loved the airplane ride and thought that the country was beautiful. But it seems that she and her parents did not think very much of the people who lived there. She came back with stories about people who were not very friendly (nobody made an effort to get to know them), who did not seem to care very much that Kim was from Canada, and who lived in ways that she thought were very unusual. There were very few foods she recognized and she had trouble finding the ones she liked.

What's more, Kim did not like any of the Teleahians of her own age. They did not seem anxious to talk with her, and when they did it was never about things that really interested her.

She said that while she enjoyed some of the towns and the natural beauty of the country, she would not want to return.

a. *Do you think Kim's description of Taleah paints a clear picture of what it must be like?*

b. *Should her observations be considered the truth about the country?*

c. *What are the most important things a traveller should remember about a country?*

d. *What did Kim do that prevented her from enjoying herself?*

e. *What might she have done to have a better time?*

f. *Do you think that from Kim's description you would want to visit Taleah?*

g. *Have you ever felt as Kim describes? Have you ever felt that someone was looking at you the way she viewed the Teleahians?*

h. *What do you think the Teleahians thought of Kim?*

A KID LIKE RONNIE DELO   Peter Braeger

Just as the huge gray bus was lumbering to a stop, it began to rain again, that cold, dreary, September kind of rain that dispels all thoughts of summer and makes one worry about a long, cheerless winter. There seemed to be quite a few people taking that Trenton Avenue bus home, for as the doors of the vehicle swung open, a dozen grade eight students clamored for the first seats on the bus. To the rear of this mob waited a similar number of nervous seventh graders, a handful of old

ladies with shopping bags, and one grade nine student,
Bill Casey. This young man was wiping his glasses with
his shirt sleeves and talking amiably with one of the
seventh graders, Jim Rockwood, who lived just three
houses down the street from Bill.

As they boarded the bus Jim noticed that the aisle was
overflowing with people not yet sitting down. "Aw,
gees, we gotta stand," he moaned. "All the way to the
back," growled the driver. Jim and Bill headed in that
direction, and to their dismay saw that no seats were
left. The whole rear half of the bus was filled with
seventh and eighth graders all from Central. In the front
were a number of elderly women with shopping bags
and a few girls from St. Mary's who had already been
sitting for quite a while. "I hate crowded buses!" Bill
commented as he set his gym bag on the floor and
reached for the hand-grips. "You think you do?" Jim
returned.

The bus, which had just started, now lurched
violently to a stop to pick up more passengers, and the
boys groaned as they struggled to keep their balance.
"He's not going to put more people on this?" Jim asked.
His older friend laughed. "You should see in the
winter. We'll be shoved in here like sardines in a can."

"Got a lot of home work?" "Nope. You?" "Just
history." "Mmmm, I hated history." Bill was now
watching the new boarders of the bus. One elderly lady
with a shopping bag and a soaking wet black umbrella,
a few little girls who did not seem to know if this was or
was not their bus, a good-looking young woman to
whom an old man in the front kindly offered a seat, and
a boy who carried a Central gym bag. Bill instantly
recognized this to be one of the new grade seven
students, Ronnie Delo, a nice kid who suffered from a
learning problem and nearly incomprehensible stam-
mering. As they identified this new-comer, a few of the
grade eights in the back started whimpering, "Ronnie!
Ronnie Delo!" Embarrassed, the boy turned to them

and muttered, "Lllleave m-m-me alone!" "Oh, poor boy!" said the eighth grade student in the seat by which Bill was standing. Bill generally tried to avoid Norm Cather, a blond kid who could be very cruel and tough when he was in certain moods. "We're so sorry! Aren't we, guys?" Cather continued. "Yeah!" chorused a dozen voices so loudly that the bus driver turned around and stared for half a moment. Bill shuddered, half wishing that they wouldn't bother Ronnie. Sure, it was traditional for the older kids to give the new students a hard time — last year Bill himself had done his share of teasing — but Ronnie Delo was different. If those older kids wanted someone to bother, there were other seventh-graders on the bus they could tease who could take it a lot better than Ronnie. Ronnie was likely to get really upset.

The lady in the seat next to Cather rang the bell and rose to leave. The blond boy got up to let her out, and Bill, closest to the empty seat, moved to sit down next to Cather. He sat next to the window, Cather in the aisle seat. "Ronnie, Ronnie Delo!" Cather muttered. "Shut up!" Ronnie replied in a voice barely audible. "What's that? Did you tell me to shut up?" Cather wanted to know, clenching his fists and assuming an expression intended to show great anger. When Ronnie saw this, he backed away in fright, and Cather laughed. "Nerd," he simply said. Loud cries of "Nerd" erupted from the assorted grade eights on the bus. Bill couldn't help but smile. Maybe it was wrong to pester a kid like Ronnie, but sometimes it was funny. And yet, when he felt himself smiling, he also felt a twinge of guilt. "Do you care if I open the window, Norm?" "Do what you like," Cather said. Bill pushed on the handle and a bit of fresh air flowed into the bus. "Sure is cold out," he said. "Yeah," replied Jim, still standing. "It's supposed to go down to 7 tonight." Cather turned to the kid in the seat behind him. "Hey, Rich. How do you like Ronnie Delo's hat?" "Oh, it's real cute!" his friend remarked. "Hey, Ronnie! That hat you have there is real pretty. I really like that little tassel at the top. Did your mommy make you wear it?" Ronnie stuck out his lower lip. "He's pouting now. We must have hurt his feelings!" "Aw!" moaned the chorus again. Bill frowned, seeing how quickly these guys had forgotten how they felt just one year ago. Ronnie had now turned to face the front of the bus. Very quietly, Cather got up from his seat and tiptoed behind him. All it took was a fast snap of the wrist and the 'cute' head covering was in Cather's hands. "H-h-hey!" Ronnie whirled around. "Whoa!" Norm shouted. "Hey, keep away!" He flung the hat in the direction of the back of the bus, where it was snatched by one of the other kids and hidden from sight. "G-g-g-ive him back his hat!" Cather stammered, duplicating rather closely the pitch and tone of Delo's voice. "Smith, pass it up here!" As the hat flew past Bill, he was tempted to grab it and flip it back to its owner. But Cather reached it first and tossed it to the rear of the vehicle again. "C-c-c-ome on!" Ronnie complained every time the hat was within his grasp, but always it was kept just from him. Then, one eighth grader in the back threatened to drop the hat out the window. When he opened the window and held the hat out, Bill could see tears welling in Ronnie's eyes.

Now Bill wondered if this game had not gone far enough. In the first place, it was cruel to bother a kid to tears, and to so badger a kid like Ronnie Delo was even more wrong. But what could he say to make them give the hat back to its owner? They knew the practice of teasing all grade sevens, and they regarded Ronnie as just another new student. To tell grade eight kids to quit taunting him would seem rather strange, especially coming from an older kid. He would be endangering his reputation, at least come out looking rather foolish. Wasn't he a grade nine student? Would not the eights do whatever he asked? He looked at the faces of the wild eighth graders. There would be no telling what he could expect unless he asked them to stop.

Bill thought hard. Then, almost without knowing it, he stood up, planning to address the grade eights and terminate their cruel game. Bill was suddenly aware of the sweat on his palms. Even with the window open, he still felt very hot. Struggling for words, he imagined that the eyes of everyone in the bus were upon him. Still his tongue fought to find his message.

Cather looked up at the standing boy. "Oh, sorry, is this your stop?" "Ummn, hummn, no," Bill Casey said. "Ummn, I, er, that is, I just wanted to, unh, stretch my legs a little." "Oh," Cather said in a disinterested tone. He went back to trying to get his friend to drop Ronnie's hat.

Now Bill was feeling like a fool, and he sat back down. To be a hero now was going to take more courage than he could get together.

Fortunately, the hat was not let out of the window and now it was once more going from person to person all over the back of the bus. Ronnie was almost in tears as he pursued it in vain. At last he managed to get one hand on his hat, but the leading antagonist also had a good grip. Ronnie tried to shake Cather loose. "L-l-let go," he demanded. "Make me!" replied Cather in a challenging tone. Ronnie stared him in the eye. "You . . . !" he swore.

For an answer Cather rammed his first into Ronnie's face and at the same time let go of the hat. Ronnie staggered backwards from the force of the punch and the sudden change of the pull on the head covering. Bill gasped, surprised that Cather would hit the kid. Ronnie wiped his bloody nose with the object of his trouble, and, finding a seat at last, sat down. But Bill could feel the pain.

He and Jim left the bus at their stop. On the walk home from there Bill was lost in thought. "Boy, am I glad I'm not Ronnie Delo," Jim was saying. "Cather really laid one on him!" Bill hardly heard him. His conscience made him feel like an accomplice to the crime. "Well, I'll see ya tonight, probably," Jim said, turning into his driveway. "Right," Bill returned. "We've got that hockey practice tomorrow." "Maybe we can go together," he added, trying very hard not to think of the day's events on the bus ride home. But Bill knew it would be a long time before he would be able to forget.

As a follow-up we have a list of questions which cover the issues presented in this story. You may wish to simply discuss them or have people take on roles from the story. If you decide to role-play, use the questions as a guide to the issues you would work with.

> *Did Bill have a responsibility in this story?*
>
> *Was he right to think of intervening?*
>
> *Was he right to sit down without pursuing his goal?*
>
> *What do you think might have happened had he carried through with his plan? How might Cather have reacted? How would Ronnie Delo have felt?*
>
> *Do those who took part in the teasing share a responsibility for what happened to Ronnie or does it rest only with Cather?*
>
> *Do you think that any of the teasers might have felt as Bill did just before he stood up? If so, why did nobody show it? If not, why was Bill the only one who objected?*
>
> *Have you ever known a Norm Cather? Have you ever behaved like a Norm Cather?*
>
> *Why do you think Norm teases Ronnie? Does he get anything out of it?*
>
> *Why did he hit Ronnie?*
>
> *Have you ever been in a situation similar to the one described in this story? How did you react?*
>
> *Imagine you are in Bill's position. What do you see yourself doing?*

Imagine you are one of the passengers on the bus. Would you become involved?

Will Bill think about this incident very much?

Will Ronnie Delo?

Will Norm Cather?

Will the kids who teased Ronnie?

Will the passengers on the bus?

Would you if you were Bill?

What do you think might happen the next time Bill meets Ronnie Delo?

How would both of them feel about such a meeting?

What about the next time Bill sees Norm Cather?

How might events in this story be changed so that Bill is able to carry through with his wish to stop the teasing?

WHITE MICE

This is a true story.

Imagine you are invited to a party. A lot of kids you know and like will be there. So you are really looking forward to it.

You get there a little late and a group of kids are in the living room with an older boy you (and most of the others) do not know. As you come in he is saying, "This is really interesting. So you think that *you* have actually seen *white* mice." A boy replies, "Of course, I have. We had them in school, and then I saw them in a pet shop. Lots of them." The older boy asks, "Were they in a box or cage marked 'white mice' or what made you think they were *white?*" "There was no sign or anything! I *saw* that they were white. Ears, tails, fur, red eyes, the whole thing." "I see. Was anyone with you who suggested they were white mice?" A girl, Erica, speaks up. "I guess you have never seen white mice yourself. Have you ever seen gray or brown mice then?" "Yes, I have." "Why are you telling these kids then that they

have not seen white mice?" "Because there aren't any."
"How do you know?" Greg pushes to the front. "Are
you saying that there aren't any white *animals*? Are you
saying that they are really albinos, that it is the *absence* of
colour that makes them appear white?" "No," smiles
the boy, "that is not my point at all. I am just telling you
that there are no white mice." Gene is really getting
angry. "Look, it's you against all these kids who have
seen them. Are you telling us we are stupid or something? What's your name, anyway?" "Oh, sorry, it's
Les. I was just pointing out that we are all living with a
lot of illusions. We think the sky is blue because it *looks*
blue, for instance. But there is no blue color up there,
is there? You find daily references to the color 'sky-
blue' though. Things like that. It has never occurred to
you to question it. And you have heard people refer to
'white mice'. Have you ever seen a pink elephant?"

A boy is putting on his wind-breaker. "I am going
home to get my sister's white mouse. If I can sneak it out
of her room. She's asleep." He leaves.

You are undecided what to do. Kids are shouting at
each other. Les is not really upset by all this. In another
room they are playing records. There is ping-pong in
the laundry room. You came here to have a good time.
What are you going to do?

> Do you usually trust your own judgments?
> Was all this really about white mice?
> What is going on here?
> What is Les doing?
> Why are people so angry with him?
> What are they feeling?
> Why are they feeling these ways?
> What are they doing?
> What other things could they have done?
> How important is it to **you** to 'win' an argument?

(What happened? In the end the boy could not bring
his sister's white mouse, but Les suddenly said, "Of

course, I know there are white mice. I just wanted to see what you would do!")

Discuss fully.

THREE GOOD FRIENDS

Terry, Karin and Maria have been best friends ever since they went to Kindergarten together. They live in the same neighborhood. When they were little they used to spend a lot of time in Maria's kitchen, particularly in winter when they came in from the cold. Maria's mother was always baking something.

Before Terry's parents were divorced, Terry's dad used to take them to the ball park and play baseball with them and Maria's brothers. That was a lot of fun. Now Terry lives with her mom who is a businesswoman and works late hours sometimes. Terry is alone a lot, but she is a happy and independent girl who helps her mother. They have a good relationship.

Karin used to really love the outings with Terry's dad because her own travels all the time and she, her older brother and her mother almost never see him. She feels that she really does not know her father very well. Karin is the quietest of the three. She reads a lot and likes to listen to music. She keeps a diary.

Over the years the three girls were always very close. They had fights sometimes, there were jealousies over friendship (what friends were whose closest?), but the girls always worked it out. There were no other children their age in the whole street. Lately the girls have had some problems. They are all thirteen years old now and like to go out and do things together, like attending summer programs, going to the movies, swimming or visiting the museum or a library. When one of them is baby-sitting, the others show up to keep her company.

Suddenly, this winter, Maria is not allowed to go to the movies with them any more, if it means coming back after dark. Her dad is home recovering from an accident at work. He cannot get around yet and is really hard to be with. He yells at the older boys and the family tries to stay out of his way. His arm is not in a cast now but is still hurting and the leg is a little stiff. Maria loves her dad, and in a way she understands why he is like this, but she is also embarrassed and she does not want her friends to come to the house now.

Things have changed, she is not sure just how. They still see a lot of relatives, her cousins whom she likes, but she still feels left out of things. She feels different and somehow disadvantaged now. She cannot talk to her parents about it, and although she understands their reasons for not letting her go out as she used to, she finds it impossible to tell her friends and explain it.

One day a form is sent to all families with children in grade eight. There is going to be a whole week's camping trip to a conservation area, an outdoor education project, involving several of the teachers, adult volunteers and fifty children. As the girls are walking home they are really excited about it. They can't wait to get packing although the date is still four weeks away.

Maria is not talking. She stuffed her paper into her pocket as if she would not be bringing it back. All of a sudden, the other two stop and turn to her. "I'm sorry, Maria," says Karin. "Will you be able to go, do you think?" "Don't know," says Maria, but she knows it is not likely. "Do you want my mom to talk to your parents about it?" offers Terry. "No! That would only make it worse," says Maria and quickly walks away from them.

One followup question usually serves for this story.

How would you like to see this story end?

A PROMISE

Rolenda is a fourteen year old girl who wanted to

spend two weeks of her summer at camp. Her mother told her she could go, providing she got some sort of after-school job and raised half the money necessary for the camp fee. Rolenda managed to get some part-time work cleaning a local ice cream store and eventually saved up her portion of the money.

However, just a week before camp was to begin her mother announced that her sister and brother-in-law (Rolenda's aunt and uncle), were arriving for their first visit to the United States three days after camp was to begin. Not only did she want Rolenda to be present, but this would mean extra expenses for her and she was not sure she could send Rolenda to camp.

Rolenda, who wanted to be with her friends who were planning to go to the same camp, was very hurt and not sure what to do.

What would you advise her to do after considering the following questions? First, put yourself in Rolenda's position and then consider the issues from her mother's point of view.

    a. *Should Rolenda insist that her mother keep the promise and contribute her share of the money?*

    b. *Does Rolenda's mother have the right to tell her daughter she must stay and greet the family?*

    c. *When should a promise be kept? When may it be broken?*

    d. *How do you feel when a promise to you is broken? How do you feel when you break a promise to someone else? Is it bad to break a promise when things happen that are out of your control and do not allow you to follow through with your promise?*

    e. *Is it as important to keep a promise with someone you do not know well or are not as close to?*

HER WEAPONS   Denise Watkins

They had ignored her so long that when they did see her, she was shocked. Before she was a person who would make them laugh and cheer them up in her funny sort of way. But she got tired fast and would curl up in the corner with her clothes on and go to sleep. They didn't mind, they were tired of laughing anyway. Let her sleep, no one cares. And after a while someone saw her curled up in her corner.

"What is that girl doing there?! She should be up in a proper bed with proper sleeping clothes on."

"But she's happy there, no one cares, she's not bothering anyone."

"No! I will not have it. Take her to bed!"

So they dragged the poor girl upstairs. She was so surprised and angry that they woke her up and moved her away from her comfortable spot.

"Take your clothes off and go to bed!"

"But I don't want to, just let me be," she said.

"Don't be a baby, and do what you're told. Don't start an argument; I'm not in the mood. Go to bed! And don't look out the window!"

They slammed the door and left, and again forgot about her, but agreed it was the best thing to do.

They said they know and cared. But she says that she liked it better before, when they didn't care, and stands and looks out the window and writes down these words, which she will read to them, whether they like it or not, because her words are her weapons.

What are your 'weapons'?

How effective are they?

Why do some people need 'weapons'?

JUSTICE?

Here is an adventure in which our hero seems to be out-smarted. Working as a group, can you solve his problem?

We are unable to find out if this is a true story or not; at any rate, in a small town in medieval Europe the following is said to have happened:

A young man wandering through the land was caught stealing a lamb from a peasant who was taking a flock to market. The thief was taken before a judge who fined him ten guilders and told him if he ever set foot in this town again he would go to jail.

The young man went on his way. In the fall, returning to his own village, he came through the town at night. He intended to pass through in great haste, however, he felt so tired and worn out that he found a hayloft and decided to sleep for a few hours. While he was asleep a cattle thief was prowling around the buildings. When the dogs started barking in the homestead, the prowler was startled and spilled an oil lamp in a doorway which set the barn on fire. He quickly ran away, but the young wanderer escaped from the hayloft just in time to be caught by the enraged peasant who accused him of setting the fire.

When taken before the judge once more the young man protested his innocence. The three members of the court could not make up their minds whether he was telling the truth. They finally agreed to let the lot decide. They would put two folded pieces of paper into a jug, one saying 'innocent', and the other saying 'guilty'. He would draw one and they would deal with him accordingly. The young man picked one of the two. It said 'innocent' and they let him go on his way, promising him no mercy if he ever came before them again.

A few years passed and the young man grew older and learned a trade, but from time to time the 'wanderlust' would drive him out into the world again. He now had a horse to ride and fine clothes and he believed that no one would recognize him in the town of his former calamity.

They might not have paid attention to the stranger riding through the cobble-stoned market square if the townsfolk had not been on edge about a frightening incident: The mayor's daughter was seen riding out of town on a stranger's horse, they said, and had not been heard from in a week. In no time at all our young man found himself in jail once again, this time charged with abduction, a very serious crime. Although he was innocent, he was not hopeful. They had no evidence against him, however, they never believed his innocence the last time he came before them, and this would seem like proof that he had been a rogue all along.

When the court assembled the townspeople filled the spectators' benches. Much time was spent describing the horse the mayor's daughter was seen riding — from a distance. Much time also was spent dwelling on the young stranger's poor reputation in this town. No one was there to stand up for him. He was on his own.

As there was really no evidence once again to convict him, the members of the court agreed once more to let the lot decide; one bearing the inscription 'innocent' and one 'guilty'. Only, privately, they had come to the conclusion that this time they had to make sure he would not get away again. They would write 'guilty' on both pieces of paper. He was to draw the lot the next morning.

At night the young man could not sleep. He had a hunch that his luck was running out. Suddenly he heard a voice outside his open window.

"Psssst," said the voice, "my conscience is not letting me sleep tonight. I have come to warn you about the draw tomorrow. Both lots will have 'guilty' written on them. I can do nothing about it. Think about this. Perhaps you can save yourself." Then the young man heard steps in the night and all was quiet once more.

The next morning the prisoner did draw one of the two lots. They did both say 'guilty', but the court had to set him free anyway.

These are all the details in the story.

What did the prisoner do?

(Ask your group if anyone has heard a similar story or 'riddle' before. If so, ask this person not to disclose the solution.)

Solution to JUSTICE?

The young man swallowed the lot he drew without reading what it said. The members of the court then had no choice but to look at the other one to determine what the first one (should have) said.

BUFFALO VALLEY

(This is not a true story but an exercise in cooperative problem solving.)

Things have been getting a little better for the Indians in Buffalo Valley after years of poverty and hopelessness. A medicinal herb, 'midgy seed', was discovered growing in the valley and a big firm started an experimental project in the area that provided jobs for many Indians planting and harvesting the crop. They were paid $3.00 an hour.

At first it looked as if their problems had vanished overnight. There would be food for the families. Other supplies could be bought, plans could be made. There would be hope.

However, it soon turned out that the harvesting of this seed brought dangers to the health of the workers. It affected their lungs.

At the same time that this was first suspected by the men, the demand for the newly discovered seed was growing rapidly to manufacture a new drug. The project manager at the farm wanted to seed more land and had to bring in more workers to plant the seed. He met with some of the Indians to tell them about this and see if they could find more workers quickly. The

Indians were hesitating because on one hand they wanted to share the opportunity for an income with other Indians. On the other they were more and more concerned about the health hazards. They said they would consider the question.

The management people did not want to wait. They asked the government to bring in immigrant workers.

The people supplied by the agency *looked different*. They were blond or red-haired and had blue eyes. They came from Whitland, a small country where people had a lot of problems finding jobs and raising families. The growing season there was very short. Fish were no longer plentiful. Many young people were leaving Whitland to look for a better future elsewhere.

After they came the project manager found that only two of the Whitlanders spoke English and that most had not worked in this country before. He put them up in wooden shacks, eight to a room, and he paid them $1.00 an hour, hoping that they would not know enough to complain.

The Indians were unhappy. They had made up their minds to tell other Indians about this opportunity, pointing out the health hazards, leaving it up to them whether or not they would apply for jobs. Now the decision had been made, and the choice was taken away from the native people, and instead these others were here in great numbers. The Indians could not talk to them or understand their ways. They seemed to keep to themselves and it was hard to know what they were thinking. Management was keeping the English speaking Whitlanders away from the Indians, or so it seemed. The Indians wondered whether the newcomers had families and if so, when they would be coming. Or were the workers counting on leaving again soon? Were they aware of the health hazards in the forthcoming harvest season? Probably not. When Joe, the foreman, had first brought the workers' breathing problems to the project manager's attention, he was told that an investigation would be made promptly. They heard nothing further about it, though.

In a meeting one evening Joe, Louie and Bert are appointed by the Indians to speak with the management people on their behalf. They would have to ask about the investigation and about the Whitlanders.

The project manager has given Joe an appointment. He knows that the Indians want health protection. He has done nothing about their complaints. He suspects that any equipment to protect their lungs would cost the company a lot of money. He also thinks that the Indians will ask about the Whitlanders' wages. He must think of some plausible reasons why he is paying them so much less.

"They are inexperienced," he would say. "Also, they have few expenses. Many don't have families." Two of the Whitlanders suffered a bad case of sunburn early on working in the fields all day. He would say that they are not healthy people, not capable of dealing with this environment. At first they worked more slowly than the Indians and he would say they are lazy.

When Joe, Louie and Bert come for the meeting they are very quiet and polite. They have been chosen as spokesmen because of their patience and reason but also because of their sense of justice. They ask about the investigation of the health hazards. When the manager avoids a direct answer to their questions, they finally realize he has done nothing. The three become very angry. They feel insulted at being ignored, feel that their health is considered unimportant. They feel exploited. They decide that they will take action. They tell the manager that they will go to the Whitlanders and make sure they are fully aware of their working conditions.

The manager becomes very concerned about what will happen to his operation. He fires the three Indian delegates on the spot and tells them to leave the site immediately. He personally takes them to the bus stop. Then he goes to the English speaking Whitlanders and makes them foremen at $3.25 an hour each.

What happens next?
How do you think this situation will end?
What would be an ideal solution?
How could it be brought about?

7

Writing Exercises and Kids' Literature

Some kids are far more comfortable expressing themselves in writing than in discussion, roleplaying, and other interactive ways. Furthermore, some kids express themselves much better in writing than through other activities. We have evolved a number of directed, goal-oriented writing exercises, three of which are presented in the first part of this chapter. Such activities have resulted in satisfying written work as well as lively discussions in our classes.

We have also had a lot of success sharing and discussing peer literature in groups. It is extremely supportive to show kids stories and other writing by others of their own age. They recognize shared feelings, opinions, concerns, and experiences. It helps them to know they are not alone and that others are confronted by, and are dealing with, the same conflicts. However, as writing often also reveals very personal thoughts and emotions, we avoid showing groups the work of people they may know. We type up and either read or duplicate stories, poems, and the like, identifying the author by name only. We do not edit or otherwise improve peer literature, except for perhaps correcting spelling. We would like the effect to be, "Hey, I can write a story like *that*."

A VISIT FROM PLYTANUS

For many years there has been speculation about whether or not there is intelligent life on other planets. We have no light to shed on this question, but the idea that extra-terrestrial life might visit this planet gives a good basis for a writing activity. Following is one way such an activity can be presented to kids.

Imagine that you are a visitor from Plytanus, a far-away planet in a galaxy that mankind has not yet discovered. You have been selected by your government to visit and report on a planet in a corner of a large galaxy where you have evidence that some form of life exists. Through radio messages that you have intercepted and decoded you have learned that the inhabitants call the planet Earth. Other than that you know very little about it.

You have been selected for this job for a special reason. Your society has a great deal of trust in your powers of perception and judgment. In the past you have demonstrated a thorough understanding of the way people behave. For this reason you have been asked to file a report on this planet called Earth. It was emphasized by your government that in addition to preparing a detailed account of the society, they were particularly interested in your personal feelings and comments about the planet.

The following are among the things that you observe:
   a.   a freeway in rush hour;
   b.   a professional football game;
   c.   a cocktail party;
   d.   a seventh-grade classroom;
   e.   a senior citizens' home;
   f.   a temple, church or synagogue service;
   g.   a factory;
   h.   a harvester;

i. the government of your region or capital in operation.

Now prepare a report in the form of a journal, log or story for the Plytanus government.

ADVERTISEMENTS AND INSCRIPTIONS

Assignments like the following, although they appear simple, can be the basis for much creative thinking and discussion. This is particularly true when one kind of writing (such as an inscription) is viewed from an unusual perspective (such as envisioning an inscription as a label).

Write an advertisement for yourself.

Write an advertisement for a friend.

Change each advertisement so that it will appeal to each of several quite different groups.

Think of five unusual places such an advertisement might appear. Modify the advertisements for each place.

Ask kids to write inscriptions that would appear above the doors of a school, a factory, a courtroom door, an office building, and an apartment building. What would each say?

Then, have kids rewrite the inscriptions as 'labels,' such as might be found on household products or medicines. They should think of the purpose of the buildings, and in their new inscriptions deal with questions like these:

What are the ingredients of this building and the activities that take place in it?

Are some ingredients beneficial and some harmful?

Do some aspects require warnings to the user? If so, what warnings?

Should particular attention be given to any facet of the building and its activities by users?

Kids can write similar 'labels' for other institutions, products, or activities—parks, museums, bicycles, and so on.

DIALOGUES

The photographs on the following page can serve as
the basis for an imaginative and empathy-stretching
'written roleplay.' Show the group one of the pictures, or a similar one you find in a magazine. Let them
study it carefully. Ask them to write a dialogue between
the two children/groups. If your own group is so young
that the act of writing would be a major handicap or they
generally lack writing skills, the scene can be acted out
between sets of two children or small groups. It is
important here to switch roles in order to give everyone
at least the *opportunity* to imagine themselves in the
other person's place.

Discuss fully the dialogues or stories this exercise
produced. Be careful to avoid making negative value
judgments when talking about the feelings and possible
prejudices revealed. Recapitulate what was said, for
instance in this manner: "Let's see. Toni thought that
the smaller boy was from another country; Karen said
he came from a big city like New York. All of you
discussed your favorite sports and games. Toni said
that people in Mexico don't know how to play hockey.
Mark made the point that he didn't know about that,
but that they have very good soccer players, and then
he talked about games he likes." Make sure you stress
all the points in which the children showed a sense of
sharing.

FRIENDS AND ENEMIES
Wayne Newhook

It was early winter. I had just moved into our new
house. I didn't have any friends.

I saw some kids playing snowball fights. I wanted to join in. I was starting to walk towards them to make friends, but by accident they threw a snowball at me.

I didn't think that they wanted to become friends with me. They ran towards me. I was afraid they were going to come and beat me up. I was too scared to run away. When they got close to me they apologized. They asked me if I wanted to join in the game. I said "yes".

I was on their team. I threw a snowball in the other team's face. I was so scared because I did not know them. I ran to say "I'm sorry", but he ran home.

I went home to tell my mother that I had made some new friends. She said, "That's good!"

Then I told her that I had enemies, too.

A BAD DREAM
Michael S.

I wake up and I am a Polar Bear in Florida. All the people are running after me waving guns, and no one of my own kind to stand up for me, everybody convicting me without a trial. I am scared. I run in the woods but they are all over the place.

Then I wake up. My sister says, "Wake up, stupid."

Write a. A Bad Dream
      b. A Good Dream

TWO HAIRY BEASTS
Christopher A. McAdam

Once upon a time, in a magic forest, there was a beast. This beast was hairy, fat, stupid and ugly. One day this hairy, fat, stupid and ugly beast was hopping around in the forest singing, "Tiptoe through the Tulips".

He looked up and saw a big tree, so he climbed it. When he was at the top he felt he would like to do something kind of bad to somebody. Just then another hairy, fat, stupid and ugly beast came along. "That hairy, fat, stupid and ugly beast is just what I want," said the other beast. Right when the other beast was walking under the tree — oh yes, I forgot to tell you their names. The beast in the tree was called 'Stupid' and the beast on the ground was called 'Hairy'.

Back to our story. The beast that was walking under the tree started to feel little things hitting his body. He thought it was rain but it was really Stupid spitting on Hairy from up in the tree. Then Hairy walked one step back and Stupid heard something crackle. He looked at the branch he was sitting on. It was starting to break. Then he heard something, and the branch said, "Get off of me, you stupid, fat, ugly beast!" And before Stupid could say, "Okay" the branch broke and Stupid fell on Hairy.

(How would you like to see this story end? The one by **Christopher A. McAdam**, in MAKING WAVES, Books By Kids, goes on like this:)

Luckily Stupid was a boy and Hairy was a girl. They looked at each other and Hairy said to Stupid, "You're cute, you hairy, fat, stupid, ugly beast." "Well, thank you, I try to look my best," said he, and then they fell madly in love and walked away in the moonlight.

(Discuss fully.)

NO GIRLS ALLOWED

Charles Morgan

One day when Sally was in bed she heard something. She looked outside. There were a couple of boys building a fort and she didn't notice the **NO GIRLS ALLOWED** sign. She came down and said, "Can I help?" and the boys said, "NO. You'll put curtains on our window and besides, can't you read?" "Yes," said Sally and she ran home and she got mad. Then she rounded up some girls and built a tree house.

The boys said it was great to themselves. They said, "We should have built a tree house but it's too late now. We already finished it and have no more wood. The girls have a light and everything, just like a real house."

(How would you like to see this story end? The story by **Charles Morgan**, who is nine years old, goes on this way:)

The girls saw the boys' lips move, so they knew they were talking about the neat tree house they had built. The boys became jealous and got some more wood at the lumber store and made something better on their fort. The girls saw and they made something better on their tree house. It went on and on until the girls saw something that they did not know how to build. The boys saw something that they did not know how to make. They were scared to ask each other, then they did.

They showed each other and they both said they wanted to share the fort and the tree house, and that is what they did!

BUT THAT'S NOT HOW I FEEL
Joelle Hétu

Other kids feel scared
But that's not how I feel.
Other kids feel stupid
But that's not how I feel.
Other kids feel smart
But that's not how I feel.
Other kids feel pretty
But that's not how I feel.

Other kids feel ugly
But that's not how I feel.
Other kids feel dumb
But that's not how I feel.
Other kids feel ignored
But that's not how I feel.
Other kids feel sad
But that's not how I feel.
Other kids feel bored
But that's not how I feel.
Other kids feel happy
But that's not how I feel.
(I don't know how I feel.)

How do you feel?

CHARLIE

Paola Argentino

Charlie was a very special person,
He tried to love people.
Oh, how he tried.
But how could he love someone,
Who didn't give a damn about him,
Who played dirty tricks on him,
Then laughed till tears streaked their cheeks.
Charlie laughed along trying to understand,
To love them.
Charlie needed love,
But there was no one there to give it to him.
He knew it.
Charlie died at the age of thirty-three,
He was laughed to death.
I know,
I laughed.

8

Low-Competition Outdoor Games

Outdoor games with a low competition component provide the opportunity for all children to join happily in physical activity without the pressure of having to be a 'winner.' These ten games require no special equipment or markings on a playing field. An outdoor space plus a soccer or playground ball are all that is required. As children become familiar with these low-competition games you may want to work out a new game following these as models.

GREEN

Children form a circle. One holds a handball or soccer ball. As the ball is thrown to another child in the circle, the thrower calls out a color, such as fire-engine *red*, forget-me-not *blue*, or octopus *black*. The receiver must catch the ball and then takes a turn calling out a color and throwing the ball to another child in the circle. If the color is *green*, however, the receiver must be careful not to catch the ball but to let it fall to the ground. The objective here is not to weed out slowpokes, but to invent new crazy-sounding colors and to have fun! End game any time.

THIRD CHILD RUNS

Children line up in twos, not as if to march in a column, but as if to be inspected by a visiting dignitary, facing to the front. They then step one yard apart to leave room between them. Two children stand in front of this formation, one is the 'runner' and the other the 'catcher'. The 'catcher' has to try and touch the 'runner' on the shoulder, at which point they switch roles. The 'runner' runs in and out between the line-ups to avoid the 'catcher'. The 'runner' can save him/herself by suddenly standing still in front of a two-some. When this happens the child in the back row must quickly run from the 'catcher' because he/she is now the 'runner'. When caught, roles are reversed again. End the game when all children have had at least one turn at either role. When children are thoroughly familiar with this game and its rules, it becomes fast and exciting, a favorite often replayed.

TREE BALL

This game can only be played in an area where there are a good number of mature trees standing close together. Each tree receives a 'defender'. A soccer ball is placed on the ground and a 'ball boy/girl' is chosen. The 'ball boy/girl' tries to kick the ball to a tree and hit it. 'Defenders' try to fend off the ball, can run around the tree, wrap themselves around it, anything, so long as they stay in physical contact with the tree at all times. When the tree is hit by the ball, 'ball boy/girl' becomes 'defender' of it and 'defender' becomes the new 'ball boy/girl'. End game any time.

KEEP IT OUT

Children form a circle, standing with legs just far enough apart to let a soccer ball through. One player outside the circle runs around with the soccer ball and tries to surprise people by suddenly tossing the ball in through legs. Children in the circle cannot bend knees or kneel down, but only use their hands to keep the ball on the outside of the circle. The ball may not be tossed in between children, only through the legs. When successful, the player outside the circle changes places with the one who let the ball through. End the game when each child has had a chance to be 'outside player'.

JUMP THREE TIMES

Two teams line up facing each other, approximately 15 to 20 yards apart. In the middle between them a stick or rock or other item marks the 'spot'. The first player of Team A throws a handball or soccer ball to Team B and starts running towards the 'spot' as fast as he/she can. At the 'spot' he/she jumps up and down three times before returning in a zig-zag line to the team line to avoid being hit by the ball. If someone on Team B caught the ball this player tries immediately to hit the runner of the opposite team while at the 'spot' on the way back to the base line. If the runner is hit, he/she has to change over to the other team. If not, the unsuccessful thrower has to change teams. Now the first player of Team B throws the ball and runs towards the 'spot', trying to avoid being hit before returning safely, etc. The game ends when all players are on one side, but it can be ended any time to de-emphasize 'winning'.

DRIVE BALL

This game requires a lot of space. A large field or open area is best. Two teams of 5 to 10 players each face one another, approximately 10 yards apart. A soccer or handball is thrown by a member of the first team in the direction of the other team. The objective is to catch this ball every time. When the ball is caught the catcher may take three large steps in the direction of the opposing team to throw the ball. If the throw is high and/or far, the team will have to quickly retreat to catch it where it comes down. If not caught, the ball is thrown from the spot where it hit the ground or a player's hand or body. Younger or smaller children have a special role to play. If a good thrower picks up the ball and the opposite team runs back to be in catching position, the ball can quickly be handed to a smaller member of the team who may not throw the ball as far but will prevent a catch. The ball should be given to team members who seldom make a catch, so they will be involved. Only the catcher has to take the three steps and make the throw him/herself. This game usually goes on forever, particularly when the teams are even, with teams moving back and forth across the field. However, whenever one team is pushed to limits of available space, coordinator may join for a few minutes to help keep game going. End game whenever everyone is tired.

CAPTAIN, HOW DEEP IS THE WATER?

Here is one of the games that children all over the world seem to invent at a certain age. Our version is called, 'Captain, captain, how deep is the water?' It can be played on a quiet street from curb to curb, or in a field or park.

The 'captain' stands with his/her back to the rest of the group, which is lined up on the other side of the street or 8–10 yards behind on a baseline. The first child calls to the 'captain', "Captain, captain, how deep is the water?" The 'captain' answers, "Two (three, four etc.) feet (or yards)", and while he/she does, the children quickly advance from the base-line as far as they dare before he/she claps and turns around to catch anyone moving or wiggling. If the children are not standing completely still ('freeze'), they all return to the base-line and start again. The first child to reach the 'captain' takes his/her place.

End game when each child has had a chance at either role.

Invite children to think of variations to the game, stressing cooperation.

HANSEL AND GRETEL

This game is suitable for wooded or ravine locations where children can hide. Two uneven teams are formed. The much smaller one, #1, takes off a few minutes before the other, #2. The exact time would depend on the terrain.

The first team's task is to search out a suitable destination through wooded or ravine land, trailing small paper bits as hints (Hansel and Gretel style). It is allowed and a good idea to put out false leads that end nowhere, to delay team #2, whose objective is to catch up with team #1 before it reaches goal. Team #1 must avoid being seen. When first game is finished, teams may wish to switch roles and start over again.

RALLY ON FOOT

The course has to be prepared carefully ahead of time by the coordinator or counsellor. Groups of four or so leave at eight minute intervals racing against time. They have to reach a destination but must take instructions along the way from notes hidden under bushes or poked onto tree branches. These may include directions as well as tasks such as collecting acorns, pine cones, maple leaves or other items (beer bottles or pop cans, if the area is polluted). Last group must also collect all bulletins along the way.

TREASURE HUNT

This is the familiar and popular game where two teams are directed to a point of destination known to all through wooded or ravine area, but via different approaches, each marked by linen strips tied to twigs, arrows scraped in dirt or marked on path with chalk. False leads are allowed but must be equal for both teams. Finally, at the goal, have the 'treasure', a container with lemonade, raisins or peanuts available.

Afterword: Dealing with Namecalling

Say it is the end of the day and you and they are on their way home. The temptation to ignore the whole thing is definitely there. They *want* to go and so do you. This is the best time to tackle it, so there is an immediate consequence to what was done.

You call a meeting right on the spot, only involving those doing the name-calling, those being insulted and witnesses, no spectators. Form a circle, make them *face* each other and you. Rather than lecture, try to make your statements in the form of questions to the kids: "What made you so angry that you just called Billy a name?" If there is no answer, ask another question, "Was it Billy who made you angry, Rob, or what happened? Was it something else?" You may have results at this point.

As we all know, kids will pick on low-status peers to let off steam, to get rid of frustrations, without provocation from these peers. So dig for the cause *that day*. Listen patiently and sympathetically. You will notice that the insulted kid is also listening with interest. If nothing comes from the name-caller, turn to the injured party. "Billy, how do you feel when someone calls you a 'fatso'?" He may not answer your question but say instead, "Oh, I just ignore name-calling. That's just stupid!" If the kids are very young Billy will say with great emphasis, "But I didn't *do* anything, I was just putting on my coat!"

If all those involved in the incident are not talking, turn to the 'black sheep' in the group, the bully, the one who gets his attention by doing something disruptive. "Peter, perhaps you can describe how this whole thing started?" Look confident and expectant that he will, and be prepared to listen. He may or may not supply his version of what happened, but the others will immediately come to life now and interrupt, because they share a low opinion of his ability to handle this. Do not let them take over. If he is not talking, wait for him to put it together. The peer protest may challenge him into action. If he is telling his story, listen carefully, then re-cap to him, without implied judgment, exactly what he said. Sample: "I see, Peter, you say that Billy pulls his coat off the hook, so others' things fall on the wet floor." Turn to someone else. Again, listen carefully, then re-cap. And so on. Never neglect to help the offending kid clarify his position and feelings. Paying *more* attention to the injured party makes his or her position in the group more vulnerable. Billy will find out that kids get angry when they find their things on the wet floor; the others will discover that Billy is in a tremendous hurry to get away, so he can run home before others bother him. Also, he was not *aware* of what made them so angry.

Without your putting it into words, it should become clear to everyone that this incident started over a minor matter. Let them discover how important it is to tell people when and why we are angry. Be prepared to teach them how to do this constructively. Then let them go.

If namecalling occurs when kids are on their way into your room or the activity you are leading, what do you do? You would much prefer to get going with what you had planned to do. But we believe the activity you prepared is very unlikely to receive much attention under the circumstances. Emotionally preoccupied kids are in poor condition to sit quietly and concentrate. It is wise to help them with their hurt feelings or anger first, and then turn to the activity.

On another occasion, not at this time and not the same day, talk with your group about name-calling in general. If you are slim, tell them they used to call you 'stupid fatso'. If you are on the rotund side say they used to call you 'dirty beanpole'. If you are known as an athletic person, tell them they used to call you 'the ugly bookworm', and so on. Discuss *your* feelings at that time. Everyone present will be able to identify with them, very much including name-callers. They invariably have bad feelings about themselves and do not enjoy their own roles.